DAFYDD EVANS
FYNNONHENRY

AUTHOR
REV BENJAMIN THOMAS (MYFER EMLYN)

TRANSLATION
CYRIL TREHARNE

COMPILED BY
C.P. REES

First published in Great Britain 2020 by C.P. Rees

Bethesda Chapel, Narberth, Pembrokeshire

Text Copyright © 2020

ISBN: 978-1-9995850-9-9

Cover design by Rebecca Tadman

Design by Design Marque

Printed and bound in Great Britain

On behalf of Bethesda Chapel Narberth, our grateful thanks to the family of the late Mr Cyril Treharne for giving permission to publish his translation of Benjamin Thomas (former Minister of Bethesda, Narberth) account of the life and ministry of Dafydd Evans Ffynnonhenry.

This book is dedicated to the memory of Cyril Treharne with appreciation to the family for their support to the cause of Bethesda Chapel Narberth.

Remember those who rule over you,
who have spoken the word of God to you,
whose faith follow, considering the outcome
of their conduct.

Hebrews 13.7

TABLE CONTENTS

PREFACE

I have tried, while translating Myfyr Emlyn's (Rev. Ben Thomas') biography of Dafydd Evans, Ffynnonhenry, to keep as near to the text of the original biography as possible. I feel sure that the reader will come to understand why I have done this. The reader will undoubtedly realise that Myfyr Emlyn was a master of hyperbole, a lover of long, convoluted sentences and the over use of some very odd Welsh idioms. But in spite of all this I believe that the reader will also learn a great deal about, a very interesting, natural character who could be said to be unique, and well worth knowing. In the Bible we come across a unique character in the person of John the Baptist; in this biography we find a truly peerless, rural, Welsh character of a by-gone era - Dafydd Evans, Ffynnonhenry. I sincerely hope that by reading this book you will agree that it has been worth my while to translate the original biography that was published in 1870.

Ffynnonhenry Chapel

Around the year 1730, when a Mr. Enoch Francis who was working in the chapel at Newcastle Emlyn along with a Mr. James James, was invited to preach in a farm called Nantgwyn, near the village of Llanpumsaint. This led him to be invited to go there on numerous occasions. Before long many of the people of the area were baptized and became members of the chapel at Newcastle Emlyn. Over the next few years the membership increased as well as the number of 'listeners'. This led to the chapel that became known as Ffynnonhenry, situated a short distance on the right off the Llanpumsaint-Cynwyl Elfed road, being built about 1735. It was called Ffynnonhenry because nearby there was a well of that name.

The chapel stands in a very steep-sided valley - an idyllic spot, and the silence is such that it can be felt and heard. The chapel is typical in design to the non-conformist chapels of Wales, and stands on solid rock. Running through the churchyard is a stream, and this adds to the beauty of the location. The chapel was rebuilt in 1828, this fact recorded on a stone tablet on its front, that reads, "This chapel rebuilt in 1828 by James Davies and David Evans, Ministers, and John Williams and Evan Evans, Deacons." The graveyard is divided into three sections by both a stream that runs through it and a narrow road that runs parallel to the stream. On the other side of the road the graveyard is on a very steep slope, and taking a coffin up to a grave must have been both a difficult and dangerous task for the bearers, especially during frosty weather. Many ask why the chapel was built in such an isolated spot, well, at the time it was first built freedom to worship was far from what it is like for us today. Nonconformists suffered persecution, and scattered all over Wales there are similar chapels built in similar locations because of this persecution. It is a recorded fact that people met to worship in caves and under trees. Such a cave is located between Llanpumsaint and Pencader.

Dafydd Evans, Ffynnonhenry 1778-1866.
Myfyr Emlyn - Parch. Benjamin Thomas, 1836-1893.
Translated in 2009 by Cyril Treharne from the Welsh version,
published in 1870

INTRODUCTION

I believe that everyone will realise that he is a strange character, worth looking at, and keeping in mind, and it would be a great pity if he was to become forgotten in 'the valley of the deepest darkness.' as has happened to many worthwhile and important characters who are no longer with us. I do not think that there is a better, constructive and more interesting, valuable and sacred biographical literature than that provided by Dafydd Evans in fulfilling its purpose, which is to bring Dafydd Evans as he was to the reader - without being guilty of taking away, as Delilah took away Samson's hair, the true story about Dafydd Evans. It is not my aim to make an angel out of a donkey; but to show clearly what kind of man he was, without giving him undue praise or point out any of his faults. As to whether I have succeeded it is for the reader to judge.

It is possible that the charge of lack of order will be made against the book, but I want to point out in my defence, whether it is wise or otherwise that this is intentional; but I believe that the reader will see a purpose in what I have done when he has read the book. I did worry to a certain extent that there are weaknesses in it, but after noticing them, I am not at all inclined to make any changes, but to throw a suitably warm cloak over it all. Kind reader, will you do the same?

I do not believe that there is anything in the book that lowers the taste nor weakens grace - to the contrary; it is to exalt and encourage imitation, and the reader feels a greater inclination towards nature, heaven, and God's sparks that fall from the altar of the 'old Ffynnonhenry' after reading the book, warming the heart. I trust the seed will be dropped in many fields, until producing many a natural and self-producing character who will once again enhance, strengthen and decorate Welsh Rhetoric, as in days and years gone by... With this preface, I present this book for the attention of man and the support of God.

B. Thomas, Pentre Farm, April 19th 1870.

Chapter 1
Dafydd Evans

Far too often it is taken for granted that Welsh oratory has stood still since the time of Christmas Evans, Williams of the Wern, John Elias etc - that the tide of ministry ebbed after their day - that there has not been anyone that could be called great, humorous, and original after them; but this is undoubtedly a mistake; some even greater and some of equal ability have followed them. There is no one perhaps, achieved as much in comparison to the darkness and hunger of the ministry of their day. The outlook of the church in that time, so short of stars, that it appears as if a great deal of attention was drawn towards them, leaving an impression on the minds of the populace so that it is difficult today to get away from hero worshipping and remembrance of other great and famous people. Following them, the stars of the ministry have been as numerous and brilliant, and the increase in biblical knowledge such that the impression is given that the ministerial talent is not as deep, lively and long lasting. The same can be said about every great and strange influence, that it lessens as it becomes more common. Do not think for a moment that I am detracting from the ability of the three referred to earlier, nor spoil their evergreen laurels, no, far from it - they were great people, people of their age, and people that will be remembered by future generations. But it should be remembered that success is not to be measured at all times by popularity. Many a rose has spread beauty and aroma in the solitude of the desert as well as in the publicity of the garden.

I will lead you now, reader, to one of the 'old fathers' who was most humorous and original, who appeared as a preacher in our country, and although he is a contemporary of many who are in some respects more famous than he is, yet possessed such peculiarity and ingenuity that he has outlived many of them, and he is a proverbial household name throughout Wales, especially in south Wales.

Dafydd Evans belongs to the present and also to a past age. He was born around 1778; when Christmas (Evans) was a 12 year old lad, working in Tynewydd, Llanfihangel Iorath, Dafydd Evans first saw the light of the sun in a farmhouse called Nantyfen, in the parish of Cynwyl Elfed, Caarmarthenshire. The reader who is familiar with the task of travelling from Carmarthen to Newcastle Emlyn knows what kind of scenery surrounds the area, and what kind of geographical influences nursed his talent and gift. His father and mother's names were Stephen and Jane Evans. His mother was known both before and after she married as Shoned. Shoned Nantyfen was a very religious person; but this was not the case with Stephen Evans, and because of this he had great difficulty in getting her to agree to marry him. Boys and girls of that age were extremely careful that they married a person holding similar beliefs, but very little notice is given to this nowadays. It seemed that the main aim of the girls was to get a husband, and today it seems it is the boys who look for a girl to marry. Great benefit would come to society if connections between man and woman were based on religion and godliness. Shoned Nantyfen liked Stephen Evans in every way except that he was not religious; Stephen realised why she would not marry him, and according to some of the old people of the district Stephen Evans on seeing Shoned walking towards him would go on one knee and pretend that he was praying, and by using this tactic succeeded in getting her friendship, and eventually had her to agree to be his wife; but it seems that the spirit of prayer deserted him once he achieved his aim and was married to Shoned. Stephen Evans was of a genial and kind disposition, but totally contemptuous about matters to do with the other world, and he remained the same until he died. Dafydd Evans recounted the following tale about his father who was in a prayer meeting in Cwmduad. "There was in the meeting an old man named 'Shon y gwehydd', and his prayers were very long. In the prayer he would use unusual sentences that he used time and time again, so that the listener knew exactly how far away he was from the 'Amen'. Among other things, he would say, 'Lord, remember your church; let not the wild boar from the forest burrow into it; let her remain settled as long as the sun is in the canopy above;' and he would then shout, 'let the same happen here tonight as happened in the house of Cornelius long ago.' It was an extremely cold night, and Stephen Evans was present, and 'Shon y gwehydd' as usual was long on his knees as well as long-winded. 'Malen,' whispered Stephen in her ear, 'isn't Shon about finished yet? It is very cold here.' 'O no, poor thing,' said Malen, 'he is nowhere near Cornelius' house yet.' 'Well,' said Stephen, 'I won't go there with him tonight,' and away home he went."

Dafydd Evans was the only child of Stephen and Jane Evans, Nantyfen. His mother died when he was very young, and it was not long after that his father married a Mary Howells,

Troedyrhiw, near the village of Cwmduad. 'Pal Troedyrhiw', as she was called, was also a very religious person, and she was a tender stepmother to Dafydd, and loved him very much. After marrying Mary Howells Stephen Evans was very comfortably established because he inherited through this second marriage Troedyrhiw Farm as well as many other small properties, so that Dafydd had every advantage in education according to the standards of education in those days. He attended for many years the school run by Mr Arthur Evans, Cynwyl, who was grandfather of the Rev. A. Evans, and he was considered in the district as a bit of an academic. We do not know of anything of great significance happening to him in the days of his childhood and his adolescence.

As a boy he was looked upon as pleasant, amiable, unusual, and competent in innocent games, by his contemporaries. He would often refer to lucky escapes he had as a child. 'When I was a small child I fell into the river, and was carried down river by the water, but I came out unharmed, although there was no one with me except Providence.' 'While going to get lime in a cart, the leading horse turned sharply, and the cart fell on to its side and I was thrown over the hedge with the reins still in my hand, but I did not suffer a scrap, and neither did the horse.' 'On another occasion the cart, loaded with large pieces of wood, turned over and I tumbled out along with the timber; the two wheels came off the cart.' But Dafydd was uninjured. 'My father was very annoyed, and if the 'regulars' were around then I would have enlisted immediately, because I could not have avoided what could be classed as a misfortune. If God will be as careful

in looking after my poor soul, it is likely I will eventually be safe.'
I do not know for certain when he started thinking about his
soul; he must have been around 29 or 30. It seems that it was by
reading a book by the 'Bardd Cwsg' that his interest in eternal
matters started, and undoubtedly it influenced him mentally,
and directed him towards his undiscovered talent. He became
frightened, even without hope, on realising his state as a sinner;
it was noticeable for a long time that he looked sad and worried;
he would often wander on his own in the fields around his home,
and he was fond of the outdoor and the banks of rivers. One day
his father called with Jacki'r gof, Cwmduad, and asked him, 'Did
you see our Dai hereabout?' 'He was in that field not long ago.'
was Jack's reply. 'I am afraid he will do something to himself,'
his father said, 'he is looking very melancholic, while hunting
the other day he turned his gun on his dog, shot it, and then
smashed the gun, I don't know what is troubling him.'

But there was more than a hunting dog and a gun troubling
Dafydd, and the most careful and keen-eyed members of Seion
realised this also. Malen dywyll, an old, and very religious
woman from Cwmduad, knew exactly what was troubling him.
There was a prayer meeting in Dolgwm, and Dafydd Evans went
there; Malen dywyll whispered to Evan Tynewydd to throw
out his net, and possibly he would make a catch; their eyes in
reality were upon Dafydd Evans; but that night he escaped the
net. His complaint was not yet bad enough, nor the wound
painful enough, nor the bait tempting enough. When Evan
Tynewydd said that there was a fellowship afterwards, Dafydd
Eavns was dragged out like a fish with the hook in his mouth,

and with that, Evan went down on his knees, praying aloud, 'Lord, go after him, go after him, knock him over, Lord, knock him over for your name's sake;' and his prayer was heard because Dafydd Evans confessed to Malen, the following day that he was forced to fall on his knees before reaching 'the little stream of Dolgwm', and another three times before reaching his home at Troedyrhiw. A good practice by old religious women in days gone by, instead of gossiping from house to house, and 'throwing the children's bread to the dogs', was to search for souls who had been hurt by the arrows of the Word, and catching old 'fish' who had been stung by the drops of the ministry, that fell in Sion, and to announce everywhere that 'this person or that person had been born again.'

Dafydd Evans was pressed very hard by a 'mountain of conscience' and shaken by 'thunder and earthquake' and caught in the fear of God, and so was saying with Moses, 'I am fearful and I tremble.' He had such a realisation of himself as a sinner, according to the old fashion idea that appertains to rebirth, that he felt it was impossible for him to be saved. An easier and smoother way has been discovered in this present age, but, 'narrow is the door' and 'oppressors steal it', and difficult it had been with Dafydd Evans. He was surrounded with more darkness than the darkness that fell on Egypt, and he felt a greater and more unbearable guilt than that of the worst kind of criminal, and he looked to the throne of grace to answer on his behalf his petition; he could see the guilt of sin standing between him and God like the mountains of the Alps; but suddenly while returning home from the mill seated on his cart, his troubled mind cleared with divine force on remembering the following words:

Heavier in heaven a little drop of blood/ Than sin and all its guilt./ The voice of the wounded divine heard/ Above their damning cry. On wings of faith he to another mountain fled,/ In floods of tears by the cross he knelt./ Black cloud from Divine anger fades/ Before the Atonement rays, And earth's convulsions still beneath His feet,/ And fiery lightning stifled by the blood.)

Soon afterwards he was baptised by the venerable Gabriel Rees, Rhydwylim, who often visited Ffynnon in those days. It was not long, in view of his promising talent, before he was encouraged to advise and preach in public; this he did, resulting in much approval. The famous and godly Titus Lewis, Carmarthen, attended to Communion Sundays in Ffynnonhenry, following the death of Gabriel Rees. It was not long before he was also picked out by death; and while on his deathbed the leaders of Ffynnon went to see him to ask his advice with regard to the future, and his blessing fell on Dafydd Evans, and they urged him to concentrate on full time ministry; this happened in 1811, when the Rev. Timothy Thomas, Aberduar, ministered with others, at a special service; and time proved that the advice of the venerable T. Lewis was according to the will of the Lord.

Some of the leaders of Ffynnon asked his father whether he would be willing for Dafydd Evans to be ordained, and could he go to the river to be baptised. 'Why not?' he replied, 'He goes every day up to his navel searching for fish!' he was very fond of fishing until his dying day, as we will later discover.

Very few changes and variety were noticeable in his everyday life. He married Margaret Davies, the daughter of the brother of the Rev. Daniel Davies, Talgoed, and she was very suitable for him. They had seven children, with three still alive at the present time: they had a son Howell Evans, a Veterinary Surgeon, and one of the most skilful in the profession, and one of the most genial and innocent person that was ever nurtured in the district; but he died before his father; he as a surgeon was, (as his father was a preacher), very popular in the district, and such is the memory of him to this day.

Chapter 2
The Measure of the Man

Dafydd Evans was a man of average size, with a countryman's appearance, and he was humble, and his stance had a tendency to stoop. Looking at him those who did not know him would not think that he was of outstanding ability, but to the contrary, the opposite, that he was lacking ability. Some would think that he was foolish while others took him to be wise, and he could not be ordinary in any way. It is likely that the public were for a long time unable to form a definite opinion of him: they did not know where to place him, whether to consider him a giant or a dwarf, either angelic or bordering on being half mad. He was so unique in the way he preached, that the Ffynnon and the immediate circle took a long time to really come to know him for what he was, and to know to what conclusion to come regarding him. But some observant gentlemen could see through the outward, ragged and strange appearance. The Rev. H. W. Jones, Carmarthen, was among the first to realise he had talent, and appreciate his ability, and bring him to the attention of others. Afterwards he enjoyed permanent popularity, and he was looked upon as a remarkable person in 'Judah', and as one among ten thousand.

Dafydd Evans belonged, as a man and a minister, to a family of very often original and humorous characters among different religious denominations in Wales, such as J. Jones, Llandysul; T.R. Davies; Powell, Cardiff; Robert Thomas, Llidiarde. All members of this family have been swept away from the land of the living, perhaps some of their relatives are still around; but there isn't one thoroughbred of that species in the field. Dafydd Evans was more like one of the above than anyone else we know about. Yet he stood out on his own and he was not in any way an imitator, but he was to an extent guilty of being original in all his mental impulses and fellowship. He was as original as John the Baptist. He did not attend any Academy or University, neither did he sit at the feet of any earthly Gamaliel; his academy were the forests, the meadows, creation, and his teachers were in the mountains and the rivers, the oak and the ash, the spider and the ant, the bees and the crows. To find the complete person, take him from Oxford or Cambridge. But for the original, natural, lively man take him from the desert - out of the hills of Wales. Dafydd Evans had been formed by the saw and axe, a skilful plane had never touched him, and no theological jockey placed the reins over his head to make him walk according to logical reasoning and rhetoric, and to bewilder him according to human scholarship, but it could be said about him, 'The one who made the desert a home and the wilderness his abode. He who laughs at the throng in town; will not listen to the voice of the countryside. The mountain nooks are his grass, and he searches for every blade of grass.

It does not seem likely that the Academy would agree with his philosophy. Dafydd Evans in an academy would be like an eagle in a cage or a wild ass in a field; he would soon break out into the desert, like I don't want to say anything against academies, without doubt they have done a great deal of good in many directions, but to a great extent under their rule beauty, simplicity, variations, and the world of nature is lost and instead one gets the formality, artificiality of the drawing room, and many have entered with much and come out with nothing. By going through various mills they got lost and with constant hewing by different hands they became mere wooden dust. Dafydd Evans possessed a natural talent, and it flowed as naturally as the river flows into the sea along the bed it has itself formed, and it would be wrong for any theological or classical teacher to form a new bed for it - so would be his talent like the waters of the canal, still, dirty, and lifeless. But as it was, it was a bright river, sometimes flowing slowly and princely between the green meadows, at other times running wildly between the rocks, and through the isolated valleys, sometimes deep enough to enable a ship to sail on it, at other times shallow enough that it would be possible to cross on foot. Dafydd Evans was like a walking stick that had not been carefully crafted, but more like a stick that had come directly from the hedgerow, without much decoration, the bark, the shape, the colour, exactly as it was when it was cut from the hedgerow, making one think that it was alive and still growing, and many changes would have to be done to it to make it a decorative object. He was like a fish out of water when taken out of its natural course. He thought on one occasion that he should write and read his sermon prior to delivering it. 'Well I am now an important preacher today,' he said. 'I belong to the first class. I have written my sermon, the text, and all, I need not open the Bible.' He read the sermon, but read it very clumsily; losing and missing the line at times. After finishing, one of the members said to him that he preferred the old way, 'I will preach as I want, I can never please the devils.' More than likely he had heard some complaining about his unusual method of preaching, because the best preachers often meet with the class of people who are always prone to complain. But it seems that Dafydd Evans was like David fighting in Saul's clothes when reading his sermons from a book.

When on a journey through north Wales in the company of the Rev. T. Wlliams, Ebenezer, Llangynog, they came across churches that had been influenced by the spirit of Sandimanism, and what annoyed them was to have to listen to sermons that were not solely based on the Scriptures. Dafydd Evans realised that his kind of sermons would not be appreciated and acceptable to them, and he consulted with the Rev. Williams as to what was the best thing to do, and he was advised to leave out his humorous sayings, such as, 'The man from Gadara was as full of devils as a beehive, and Christ shook them out, and they want to be tied to the swine.' 'Jesus has only to say 'Silence!' to the storm, the storm became as still as water in a pail,'

In his next sermon he dispensed with his usual pattern and put them aside, but surprise! surprise!, Mr. Williams had never heard such a poor sermon before in his life, and Evans decided leave to the Sandimanians to their opinions and he preached in his usual style, fighting with his catapult, stones from the stream, and it was rare for this method not to hit the target - the forehead of the giant, before he had finished preaching his sermon. There is nothing better than behaving in a natural way, and the chief glory of Dafydd Evans in all he did was his naturalness. He was a child of nature. He loved nature and nature loved him, and liberally opened its rooms, its libraries, and museums - throwing the best gems at his feet and whispering its secrets in his ears.

'Come, my child,' nature said, 'if you do not wander in the company of the arts and science to higher places, with their splendid buildings, and their excellent systems - if you are not allowed to enter the philosophy of the Romans and Greeks, listening to their bards singing and their orators pouring out in a flood their rhetoric - you will be allowed to wander with me along the bright banks of the river, along the quiet desert, and over the crested mountains - you will be allowed to listen to 'the heavens singing the glory of God, and the firmament showing the work of His hands.' 'I will introduce you to the animals of the fields, birds of the air, and the fish of the sea, and you will be in a league of peace with them all.'

One of the characteristics of a genius is the ability to rise above difficulties, and to lessen disadvantages, and to make everything around him work - carry out his aims - use the tongue to good purpose - feet to walk - and to be silver pipes to carry the wine to the heart. This is what Dafydd Evans did naturally. Some are forever saying, 'If I had had college, if I had had education, and if I had this or that - I would accomplish great things.'

He, possibly, had never heard of any famous pagan believers, yet he met them in the beauty of nature - the meeting tent of the thoughts of the talented of every age and country. His textbook was the Bible, and his book of reference was nature. He did not remain quiet because he could not speak in a grammatical way, but he would say what was on his mind whatever the grammatical standard of what he said, and he was always a polite Mr. Genteel whatever he said.

He was not going to be naked and starving because he could not enjoy the food of scholars, and dress in classical clothes; but he would go out in 'camel hair and his food were locusts, and white honey.' If he could not have the assistance of Engel, Alford and Ellicott, he would go to the crows, winged birds, the animals of the countryside; the pigeon came to him often, with a green leaf from the branches of the 'tree of life', and the greedy raven would bring him 'bread and meat', more often than twice a day from the table of the Eternal King.

Chapter 3
Prison

Dafydd Evans lived most of his life in Troedyrhiw, but the last part of his life was spent in Cynwyl Elfed, and although to the outside world his life was not varied there was one exception when he went to law with regards to the ownership of Troedyrhiw. As a result of losing his case in court he was imprisoned in the jail at Carmarthen for two and a half years. The exact details of what really took place have not come to light, and as a result I am not in a position to say precisely what happened, but I can say this much: 'Pal' Troedyrhiw, Stephen's second wife had in her will stipulated that he, Stephen Evans, (Dafydd's father) was to have Troedyrhiw while he lived, and to be passed on to Dafydd Evans after his days. Stephen Evans lived a very long time after his wife died, and was in possession of Troedyrhiw, and all the other properties belonging to Troedyrhiw until his death. It was after Dafydd Evans had been living in Troedyrhiw for a number of years that others came forward claiming that they were the true inheritors of the property. The matter went to law - Dafydd Evans lost the case, and he was imprisoned because he would not sign over the inheritance to whoever had laid claim to Troedyrhiw and the other properties of the estate.

There is no doubt that his step-mother thought that she had written a will, and others thought so too, otherwise neither Stephen or Dafydd Evans would have enjoyed a day after her death in Troedyrhiw without having been troubled. How it became known that it was possible to go to law regarding the matter I do not know, but it is likely that some 'cat savoured the mouse'. However, Dafydd Evans lost the case, and because the other side in the case were poor, they offered to drop it if they were paid between £300 and £400, but Dafydd Evans refused to pay. It was generally agreed by the local populace that he had every right to refuse to pay because Mrs. Evans believed that those who had advised her to do so in her will (i.e. give everything she owned to her husband and after his days, to his son) were their enemies. 'The loaf or nothing' was Dafydd Evans' response, and nothing he received. Now no one can blame Dafydd Evans for defending his rights, and the general opinion was that it should be his, but the letter of the law turned against him, and the offer of his opponents showed a defect in the law and the judgement; and in his decision to refuse to sign over his right with regard to the place, we must take into account the influences of those around him. Leaving Eden is not an easy thing to do under any circumstances, especially from the place where he had been brought up, the place where he had been born, the place where his career towards heaven began; to say the least, he went to prison a martyr to his own lack of knowledge, the influence of those around him, and his unshakeable belief that he stood for what was right.

Soon after being taken into prison the Rev. H. W. Jones visited him, believing that he was in prison because he was a bankrupt. 'In the name of God, what are you doing here?' Mr. Jones asked him. 'I do not know,' he replied, 'I do not know what for, but this is where the wicked nation brought me, and this is where I shall be in future. I will not come out of this place until I die. But in spite of their chains they cannot stop my soul from going home, it will go out when it sees fit through the roof of the old house in spite of the accursed nation.'

He believed that right was on his side although the law was against him, and whatever was the opinion of individuals regarding the effect of this on a minister of the gospel, let's remember that 'better the country than the lord', and in the opinion of the church and the country Dafydd Evans was completely innocent, and conscientious in all the discussions. Proof of this is in the fact that he went from a prayer meeting in Ffynnonhenry to jail, and on his release after some two and a half years it was to a prayer meeting and a sermon that he was welcomed with great joy back to the chapel, and to chapels throughout the country as someone who had risen from the dead. And in Seion they said, 'We must rejoice and be joyful because my son who was dead, became alive, who was lost, and was found.'

He must have been self-possessed, and with a remarkable depth of inner strength because the experience did not disturb his inner peace, nor did imprisonment destroy his happiness and blunt his godliness, but on the contrary he enjoyed much peace through his religious belief, and it seems to have increased his talent and grace more during this period than at any time during his life. He was visited by many of his old friends from many places, expecting to find him under pressure and sad but what they found was that the old prisoner was on top of the world and made them laugh for up to a fortnight after returning home.

His religious experience and inner impulses of his mind can be seen in the entries of this diary, ones that show the fountain of his comfort, and that there could have been dreadful impulses, even when he smiled affectionately and with happiness showing on his face.

"On the morning of October the 8th in bed before daybreak in prison and as I was searching for the throne of grace, I was comforted and helped by meditating the sayings of Joab and Abner in the battle 'How long before the disappearance of the sword? Joab was touched by Abner's words, and he stopped anymore blood to be shed, although he was fierce and cruel. How much better is God than Joab? It is said that the ungodly is God's sword. It is God's commandment that he return the sword to its sheath on my behalf.'"

"Another victory before daybreak in bed in prison against unbelief and doubts was on the morning of the 23rd of August, while meditating on the promises and the calling of the Old Testament and the New, such as 'Call on Me in the days of tribulation'. My sins are like a heavy load, and, 'Come unto me all that are heavy laden, and also, 'Drink freely from the water of life.' The Scriptures came to my weak heart so that they broke the back of all my doubts. Thank goodness!'"

Again, 'I had exceptional comfort on the 7th of August 1845, while meditating on the throne of grace along with the One who is sitting on it, and the large gifts that are forever given from it to poor people, and that when my spiritual poverty was coming out to meet me more like an armed giant with his brass, and his shield, and his long spear like a faction, and his leg-harness; but through help I floored him. Thank goodness!'

'12th of January 1845, in prison and my sins have become an army fighting against me all night, but it came to me with all the strength of the Scriptures: Romans 8 verse 33, the deliverance of Jonah from the stomach of hell was not sweeter. O! thanks for the mighty Word, 'God is the One that acquits.' The same authority came with these words to my weak and injured soul as came to the sailors at sea when it was said to the wind, "Silence, quieten.' As long as I live, I'll remember the place.

How sweet the Word when it comes with strength! Romans 4 verse 5 'Now to him who does not work, but believes on Him who justifies the ungodly, his faith is accounted for righteousness.' 'This poor one cried, and the Lord heard, and delivered him from all his tribulation.' Dafydd Evans will give thanks for this for ever.'

'Heaven, Purgatory, Hell. Some acknowledge these three places, everyone two of them. Similarly, there are three categories of people we have dealings with in the world when in tribulation, (1) Friends, (2) Enemies, and (3) People between the two. What the first do is rejoice in your success. The second rejoice in your fall, and grieve over your success. But as for the ones in between, they will not rejoice if you were crowned; neither would they cry if you were hanged.'

After reading the above there is no need to wonder as to the fountain of his comfort, and be surprised that even the prison was often heavenly to him. There is such a natural and striking similarity between his condition and his surroundings, that his sincerity is seen through it all. Dafydd Evans in prison was the same person as the Dafydd Evans of the 'Ffynnon'. He had light even in darkness, and freedom even in captivity. He was graceful and easy to deal with. He was not corrected for anything except for being careless with his own comfort. It seems that on only a few occasions was he reprimanded throughout his stay. He said 'Not because of any offence nor frightened of paying his dues, because the 'medicine' was free, and feeling of brotherhood quite peaceful.'

The prison chaplain came to him one day and asked him to give an account as to why he did not attend the services oftener. "Service indeed!' he replied, 'Services and church for the good you have. If the members could only find the door open they would all run out immediately.' Dafydd Evans read, prayed and gave advice so that even the worst prisoners would sober up. The prison governor said that he would very much like to keep him there permanently because it would mean that the offenders would not have to be put in the dungeon; Dafydd Evans taught better morals to them. Only God knows how much good even in prison Dafydd Evans achieved, or how much good prison did to him also. It is known that he was a better preacher afterwards. Some die and others faded because of the experiences and temptations; but others flower and bring forth more fruit. Press the grape and out comes the wine. Dafydd Evans was pressed between the walls of the prison and good. Saving wine flowed from him afterwards for more than twenty years, resulting in great joy in Zion.

His first text on his release was, "'I was in prison, and you visited me'. I could say to some, 'I was in prison and you did not visit me, but I am not going to scratch old scabs now.'

CHAPTER 4
POPULAR PREACHER

Dafydd Evans was a very popular preacher. I do not know of anyone in his time who would be more certain of filling a chapel than him; and although his name was not as well known as some other preachers, he would never travel any road twice without having a multitude following him. He was of an unique manner - so natural and original - so humorous, yet very good and simple that wherever he went, up to the mountain the crowds would follow him. When it was announced that he would be preaching in Drefach or Llandysul, or some other well-known place, even on a warm, sunny afternoon during the 'September Harvest', I dare say the chapel would be full to overflowing with people eager to listen, from the young boy to the old man - from the girl of five years of age to an old lady of seventy, and everyone would be far too interested to sleep or snooze. It is unlikely that any one would ever sleep much under his ministry, except a 'wooden man' who would not 'dance to the pipe' or 'complain when lamenting' because Dafydd Evans came to chapel to announce the 'feast that is the gospel', and 'crying in the wilderness', and not to prepare the people beds and lull them to sleep; they came not to sleep; they came especially to listen because there was something that was worth listening to. He was not like one minister who asked one of his members if he often went to listen to Whitfield, "Why," the minister said, "do you go and listen to Whitfield when I am preaching in the chapel?"

"Oh", the member replied, "you give me far too much time to think about my own life - going to the fair, and the market - tending to the cows and sheep; but when Whitfield is preaching I have as much as I can do not to miss anything he has to say." So it was with Dafydd Evans; he was proverbial in that he gave his listeners plenty to do just to listen to him relating a sermon like no one else before him about the Saviour and His talents. The eye had enough to do just looking at his strange postures, and plenty for them to do by just listening to his lively and natural sayings, plenty of work for the imagination to follow his interesting and pleasant flights of fancy, plenty of work for the taste just looking at the beautiful and eternal 'paintings', plenty of work for the penitent to enjoy the free and great forgiveness, plenty for the sinner to embrace the gracious and blessed Jesus, plenty of work for the 'new' man to eat the heavenly manna, the rich delicacies, and drink the living water that was on the table, and the 'complete' man had plenty of time to laugh often with pleasure , when listening to the rich revelation of salvation that seemed like panoramic views, one after the other, until the world and its things were forgotten and sleep retreating, even to those who at times would have a nap during a meeting.

The reader will know that the two o'clock meeting is proverbial for its tendency to sleepiness, especially in country districts, when the sleepy class are more or less strangers, enjoying the comfort and leaving the minister and the few pretending to be awake, with the health and purity of the teaching. There is a class of people that are found in every congregation that there is nothing more inviting to sleep than a sermon. They will travel three to four miles on a Sunday afternoon to have a nap! And if there was an occasion, such as the amputation of a leg or an arm, there would be no need for the doctor to bring with him his instruments, he would be able to proceed without causing any feeling, pain or danger. And this is the strange thing, these who profess that they are religious are usually in this class, and our brotherly love leads us to think that they have made their fortune, filled their vessels to the brim, and now expect their Lord while in the arms of sleep! But they lost their enthusiasm for sleep during the ministry of Dafydd Evans. There was too much 'snuff' in his sermons, that even they would not sleep. For special meetings Dafydd Evans would usually take the two o'clock service in the afternoon nearly every time if he was present, much to the disappointment of 'Mr. Sleep' because he would be denied his choice preacher.

I heard that he was preaching on a certain Sunday in a place that was well-known for sleepiness, and the minister was convinced that even Dafydd Evans would not be able to keep them awake. Dafydd Evans took two large stones with him up to the pulpit, placing one on each side of where he stood. He preached on David and Goliath. "Now," he said, "you do not know what I am going to do with these stones. Well, the first person to fall asleep will receive one of them." No one came anywhere near falling asleep, and everyone was wide awake right up to the end of the sermon; until the giant had been killed, the spoils divided, and the daughters of Israel singing the praises of the conqueror.

There is a great effort in Wales and England to bring the crowds to the 'medicine of grace' and the taking of the gospel to the 'land of the pagans'. The English preach sermons in sports stadiums, and lecture on Sunday afternoon, in order to bring the 'far off nearer to the shores of the 'lake of medicine'. Dafydd Evans's ministry was very successful and attractive in this. Among his listeners would be sinners who never walked 'in the courts of the Daughters of Sion'. The persistent swearer - the drunk and the blasphemer would be crying and laughing under his ministry' and 'playing his feather' these could soon be 'old fish that no one else had managed to get out from under the hollow in the river bank'; there is room to believe that he succeeded to hook many of them to their 'everlasting safety'.

No one left his meetings without having had something out of them, and everyone went home full of enthusiasm and all the while discussing the sermon. It would be the topic of the week by the boys while ploughing, the girls milking, the children while playing, and with the old women while knitting socks in front of the fire, and everyone would remember parts of it. There are not many preachers, now silent in their graves, that are so much talked about in country areas than Dafydd Evans. The sarcastic person can sneer, the philosopher laugh, and the scholar tut-tut, but Dafydd Evans threw enough of 'the spirit of life' to some wheels to make them turn for ages and many generations, and they will be moving in the tradition of 'the forthcoming', when the wheels of many of them will have rusted in idleness, and sunk from memory. "The one who is dead is speaking yet." There are scores throughout Wales very fond of his friendship, and love to recite his sayings. Perhaps that only ragged remains of his sermons are still to be had, but the ragged remains are not without valuable treasures in their midst. Possibly it will be 'the toads of Egypt' that is on the 'plate'. and without doubt there will be 'pearls on his lips and God in his eye.' But better the man in rags than the most splendid clothes without a man! Isn't the 'dung heap' full of pearls better than the most splendid box without anything in it? The most splendid mansion without a rich inhabitant will decay, while the white-washed cottage will stand for years. when there are healthy people living in it.

He preached in a very simple, warm and enlightened manner. One could see his thoughts observing the 'holes and clefts of his house because there was no ornate door nor windows, and the fingers of his talents moving in turn the soul from happiness to sadness.' He moved in his own light, and he would not lead his listeners to darkness. He would not guide anyone towards anything he did not understand himself, and he would never say' hear, hear' when there was nothing to hear, or 'look, look' when there was nothing to see, and 'I see first of all, and secondly' when there was nothing there but 'sickness and weakness', but he could see Jesus Christ so clearly before his eye that he could point his finger at Jesus in a most natural way, 'Behold the Lamb of God, which takes away the sins of the world.'

His illustrations were so lively and so natural, so that his listeners could visualize everything in a neat way before their eyes. He took them out of themselves, and out of the world, and he would bring them as slaves towards the shores of the Red Sea, or God's plains, or the lion's den, or Bethlehem, Gethsemane or Calvary; perhaps even to Persia, to the court of king Ahasuerus, and they could see everything clearly - the king choosing a wife instead of Fasti - the girls brought before him one by one and the king's humorous or objectionable observations he made about each one of them. There was something wrong with each one of them, but O! when Esther, the Jewish slave appeared he found her faultless; he was very pleased with her, the wheel of Providence turning from the house of Israel - Haman hanged on his own gallows so that the congregation would forget they were in chapel, but with Dafydd Evans, Ffynnonhenry, in the palace of Shusham.

A reader would notice when reading quotations from his sermons that he was excellent both at describing and also adding colour to a story. The descriptions in his sermons are so good and so true, and it is a shame for them to get lost.

He preached on 'Salvation for the many' very often. He asked, "How many? As much as was the need, as much as whoever comes, as many as for the world's wretchedness." "There is Noah building the ark, building it according to plan." "What size is the door to be?" asked Shem. "Look at the plan", Noah replied. "I've looked at the plan, but it is not there," Shem said. "Not down on the plan!" Noah said, very surprised. "No indeed," Shem said, "you look at the plan." "Well it isn't, is it," Noah said, "what shall we do now?" But after a while he said, "I'll tell you what we'll do You go down to the desert, and look out for an elephant, and note when he walks between two trees, and look very carefully and measure the height and the width when it went between the trees, and if we make a door big enough according to the measurements for it to be able to pass through then every other animal will be able to enter easily after it." "That is what we will do, dad. Great! Japheth come with me." Shem said, and away they went, and after a while they returned. "Did you see an elephant?" Noah asked" "Yes," was the reply. "Did you measure it? Noah asked. "But we saw an old creature much taller than an elephant." "O, the old gentleman will have to bend its head if it wants to enter" Noah said. The boys had seen a giraffe "Salvation as much? As much as the greatest sinner. The door is high and wide enough. The largest elephant has entered. And what large elephants were Saul, the persecutor, bloody Manasseh. They have entered. What old elephants were the Corinthians!, and another large elephant was Mary Magdalene, and standing before you at present is an elephant of a sinner. But I have sure confidence that I will be able to enter the ark. The gates of salvation are high enough and wide enough. Yes! What will happen to the Pharisees; they will never get in unless they are ready to bend and bow their heads, or remain outside. The door has not been made for them to enter with their heads up; an elephant of a sinner will enter, but the giraffe of a Pharisee without bowing his head will not. Unless you become like a 'small man' you will not enter the Kingdom of Heaven." The animals enter the ark according to their sex, and do so peacefully. O! here they come, two large snakes approaching the ark like two cartwheels. "Father, father," Shem shouts, "here come the snakes, they will surely attack us and kill us." "No, my children, they won't," said Noah, "you can play with their sting; this is a race for life, they are only trying to enter." Here come two snails, crawling in with two large castles on their backs; they set out on their journey very early, and the mole is looking for soil in order to hide. Here comes the old lion, and soon after, the fox, and following them a goose, waddling from side to side. "God help the goose," one of the children said.

After all the animals had entered the ark then Noah closed the door, but as soon as he had closed it he could hear the sound of wings beating from one corner of the door to the other. "Hello," said Noah, "who is there? "I am here," said the wren. "Why have you been so long before coming?" Noah asked. "Oh," the wren replied, "I arrived on the banks of the Jordan the same time as a hawk, and I waited for it to go in before me, that is why I have been so long." "O, there is no need for you ever to be afraid of it," Noah said, "come in, come in. Go forward next to the old bird." And there they were, all in the ark, one big, peaceful family; the lion and the lamb, the fox and the goose, the little wren and the hawk. That is how they all came to the 'Ark of Salvation' - from the east and from the west, from the north and the south; the camels of Midian, the sheep of Cedar, the rams of Naboth and the bulls of Barham, and the unicorns of Edom - one family, without one harming the other. 'They shall not hunt nor destroy in all my holy mountain. Come, come both big and small, before the coming of the flood and fire.'

Another time he preached on the resurrection of Christ:-"I was walking through a village in Carmarthenshire on fair day, and I saw two men wrestling. One had thrown the other to the ground, and doing his best to keep him there; but the man who had thrown the other to the ground and was on top of him shouted at the top of his voice, 'Push! Push!'. As I passed I asked the one who was on top what all the shouting was about; let the one under you shout, 'O, I can feel him rising, he is rising.' On the morning of the third day death was shouting, 'Push! Push!' so that all in the land of the dead were asking, 'What is wrong with you death? 'O' he is getting up, he is getting up, in spite of all my effort to keep him down.'

I have already mentioned that Dafydd Evans preached in the same manner to two or three as he would to two or three hundred listening to him, and I would not hesitate to say that that is one of the secrets of a popular and effective parson. Dafydd Evans spoke to a congregation in exactly the same way as he would talk to two or three friends while sitting by the fire, and his voice, method, movements and attitudes changing naturally to suit the subject. He was not for a moment afraid of his congregation, and the congregation were not in the slightest bit afraid of him; but showed that there was perfect understanding and sympathy between them. He was never suspicious of, nor surly to his listeners, and neither were they suspicious of him, but they understood and loved each other. He led them with a sceptre of love and rightness, and they followed him everywhere, up and down hill and dale - sea and land, until reaching the 'Amen'. When he laughed, they laughed, and when he cried they also cried. They battled together and shared together the 'booty', and suffered together and ruled together. It seems that there is a curtain between some preachers and their listeners, and speak to them through a hedge, and inside a curtain; but Dafydd Evans split every curtain, and would stand face to face with his listeners. He was able to get so close to them sometimes, that they thought he was not speaking to them, but speaking within them. He would take the hand of Jesus and the hands of the members of the congregation, so that they would all grasp each other's hands, until an 'electric shock' flowed through the congregation, and many would be ready to shout out, "Deal with me, so that I will be strengthened."

As has already been suggested, he continually fell and rose up between the sublime and its opposite. He moved a great deal between the two; he would take up in turn these two extreme opposites, without doubt, due to his natural gifts, and the different grades of his knowledge and culture. He was always perfectly natural, and he cast his naturalness and life into everything he came across. It can be said that all the wit and amusement of the denomination were to be found in Dafydd Evans, Ffynnonhenry.

He was able to dress up the humour that came to his mind was, without doubt to a great extent responsible for the fact that he was able to arrange them in order very quickly. It seems that most of his sermons were worked out - all were up to date - while walking from his home to Ffynnonhenry. They came rapidly and without warning to his mind, and he chained them to himself, and they were always ready at hand without warning. Ideas came to him without warning like chains and ropes around him, and he wore them so that they were always at hand. He would not hold events long in his mind is order that he could look at, and revise them, but used them as they were, very often not fully worked out before using them in his sermons to the congregation.

Dafydd Evans was lively and original; his imagination wild and sprightly; his feelings alive and exciting, and he had never been under properly disciplined. And so he was prone to continual extremism; he would either be happy or melancholy, serious or amusing. Rarely would he be like spring or autumn, but like summer or winter, under the heat of the equator or the cold of the poles. Some men are doleful and their looks sad, as if their Creator's purpose was to drive men to cry and to remind them of the dark side of life; while another is lively, and his manner delightful, as if he had been purposely made to make men laugh and remind them that thee is another side to life. But Dafydd Evans seems to have been purposely made to fit both types of men. He made people laugh and cry in turn; the tears would often shine through the smiles, like the drops of rain through sunshine; and then the sound of laughter replaced by the sigh of repentance, and the lamentation of the 'heart full of the plague'. He was unable to take the middle way, and only rarely travelled through the 'Middle Counties' but his pilgrimage more often on the 'frontier', near Offa's Dyke - his text affecting the mind and the emotion.

In him the extremes came together - the serious and joyful - the sublime and the offensive; and he switched from one to the other at the speed of lightning. He was like the white swan, lamenting and sad in her loneliness on the lake of trouble and tribulation;

the next second he would be like a lamb frolicking on the green slopes of the 'Mountain of the Beatitudes.' He would sometimes be the eagle flashing its wings in the vicinity of the sun; the next minute a hedge sparrow on the dung-heap. He would now be an angel enjoying delicacies, the next minute in the kitchen eating 'red broth' or 'potatoes and milk' with the servants. These sudden changes, changes that seemed strange, were perfectly normal, and in him were acceptable. He would translate his thoughts and feelings in all honesty, and he would paint scenes in a lively and homely manner, until his listeners were continually laughing or crying, and they would be surprised if he did not do both, or at least one of them.

On one occasion he was preaching and he had been preceded by a colleague who had started the meeting by reading and praying, and in the prayer had said, 'Lord, help us not say anything foolish here tonight.' In Dafydd Evans' sermon the contents were most unusual - not in his usual style - no one cried or danced as a result of what he said. Someone, who had been surprised by this, asked him why he had not preached in his usual manner; and he answered rather sharply, 'O, my brother prayed in such an earnest way for help that nothing foolish be said that I did my best for him so that he would be listened to at least once in his life.'

He would always change his tone and his posture to suit his topic; and he would also act as well as speak. Sometimes he cried, and laughed at other times, resulting in his listeners reacting in a similar way. Once he gave a picture of Jesus Christ conquering death. 'Death', he said 'ruled from Adam onwards through the ages. Only two went to the other world, Enoch and Elijah, escaping death, and they did it by slipping behind him without death knowing that they had done so. Death was always the head, and he was superior to everyone. But when the Saviour appeared, death met its master; the first time Jesus met him was in Nain. Death could be seen approaching like a big lion with the widow's son between his teeth; the way was too narrow for both to pass, and a battle ensued. 'Where are you going?' Jesus asked. 'I am taking the boy to my den', death replied. 'Taking the only son of a widow away? Don't you have any pity for her?' Jesus asked. 'Not at all', death said, 'I couldn't care less who he is.' 'Release him', Jesus said. 'What did you say?' asked death, 'Do you know who you are talking to? I am death.' Jesus replied, 'I am Life, I will make you release him.' And with this he punched him hard, and at that instant the 'old boy' put down the boy on the ground. 'Ha! Ha! That was a strong punch, wasn't it?'

On another occasion he illustrated the Son of God unravelling the work of the devil. "'The devil is a dreadful one for tying people up in knots', he said, 'But the Son of God is better at untying knots. The devil had tied up an old lady over a long period of time, for eighteen years - had fettered her so that she was like a young animal, grazing on his land. He had tied one end of the rope around her neck and the other around her feet, and she had been for eighteen years like a two-headed thicket; but Jesus Christ came on the scene, and cut the rope, and it sprung like a trap. Ha! Ha! Ha! She became as straight as the straightest young girl in this chapel. 'Now then you Pharisee, put your ruler on her back in order to see if she is straight'.

Without experiencing the presence and hearing the sermons of Dafydd Evans it is difficult to realise the pleasure everyone who heard him had when listening to him; and however lively and polished his talent is described in a book or from memory, the fact that he is not seen and heard will never do justice to him. There is no comparison between actually hearing Christmas, Williams and Elias, and a description of them afterwards; and the same can be said of all great men down through the ages. It is easier to describe talent to men than the ingenuity of the speaker. It clings tightly to 'the temple' and its old 'tools'; rarely will the consonants and the vowels together and the most charming words attract them to stay. Talent has lost its owner, like a harpist losing the harp, and having to play a violin, so it is that he longs for the tongue that spoke to him before - the eye looking through him, and the look and the action 'sharing a moment with the strong.' The stronger the talent, the more unforgettable it is in the words or the tradition of the country. It was very scarce with many; that they left nothing behind but useless 'skeletons for the shopkeeper to use for holding sugar and tea, and snuff' so that many of the houses of Seion are full of motionless wheels, and the spirit of the living thing gone, that is, if it was ever there.

Although the traditional and written remains of the old Patriarch of Ffynnonhenry are not as exciting and charming as when they happened, yet they are alive, although the one who first spoke the words is now in the silent grave. His words have become household words, and his sayings proverbial

CHAPTER 5
A ONE OFF

It is impossible for the mediocre person to successfully speak to the public; this one will take offence, another become angry, and the third scornful, but the talented can say what they like without causing offence to anyone; and one of the great things about Dafydd Evans was that no one took offence at whatever he said. He possessed so much independent thinking, good nature, and humour that he could say what he liked without causing offence. Congregationalists, Methodists, Anglicans, and others, liked him as much as people of his own denomination, although he never denied, hid or failed to defend his principles in order to please others. On one occasion, while baptising, and there were people from other denominations listening, he said, 'It is forgery to sprinkle and to name a child in the name of the Trinity. If you forged a gentleman's name in Van Dieman's Land you would be immediately condemned. I am a friend of you Methodists and you Congregationalists and others today; but without doubt you will be condemned. You are indeed wrong and should see to the matter in time.'

There were two famous Methodist preachers preaching in Cynwyl, and Dafydd Evans after hearing them preach said, "Mr. is like a big ship that depends wholly on its sails, but if he gets the right wind he moves. But Mr. is like an excellent ship, he does not depend on the wind; it is better for him if the wind is behind him, but he is certain to reach port, the wind behind him or not."

On another occasion, after listening to two very popular preachers, he said in their presence, "You preached very well, yes indeed. You, Mr. speak very quickly! A person needs to have a very strong stomach in order to be able to deal with what you feed them, you remind me of some mothers in this area who stuff gruel on the boy when he is in a hurry to go to school, 'Spoonful, after spoonful, and 'Eat boy, eat boy' until the boy is on the verge of choking, and then vomits it all back, thus losing it all. Mr. reminds of the mother feeding her baby, taking plenty of time, bit, by bit, and 'Isn't that nice, there's a big boy, it's now all finished,' and one sees the mother and baby smiling contentedly at each other. Besides the correctness of the above illustrations, they are worth 'writing down in stone,' and placing alongside gold objects.

Another time he said, 'Have you ever heard that a Jewish priest failed to understand God's thoughts, and the way to worship, although the commandments and ceremonies are countless.' 'No. Jesus commanded two sacraments on his church, and the world failed completely to understand and agree regarding them! Obvious things in the Old Testament, dark things in the New Testament! Shame if it is so with the gospel of the Son of God!' It would not surprise me if some will be offended by his remarks at that time. He did not target those considered to have strayed, but at what are considered sins - not at the sinner but at his sin. There was no poison on his arrows, or a sting under his tongue. There were people of different persuasion who were prepared to be opposed and hurt by him in order to hear what he had to say - prepared to have the bitter in order to experience the sweet - ready to have a hiding so that they could have comfort. He would attack his enemy without holding back, but the enmity would be killed by the wine of his humour: His wrath was burnt with the fiery embers of his talent; he quietened any slander because of his good nature; and the purity of his spirit stopped and healed the poison that hurt the flesh. He was also quite a wag. When burying an old lady (a member of Ffynnon), in Hermon, a Congregationalist chapel, he said at the graveside, 'Well, here is at least one religious woman lying in Hermon's graveyard.'

Dafydd Evans was as innocent and as playful as a child, and far from being destructive with his tongue, and blasphemous with his lips. I heard him say once about the tongue, "The tongue is not very big, yet is able to set the world on fire. It isn't very heavy, but many a man and woman are too weak to control it. There was once a doctor operating on a lady, but he just could not continue because of her tongue. 'Would please put out your tongue,' the doctor said. She put out her tongue, and indeed it was quite long. 'Will you hold it there for as much as ten minutes,' he said. She never had such a difficult task in her life. A tongue can be very good but also very bad. The master once sent his maid to the market to get something tasty for dinner. She returned with a cow's tongue. He again sent her to get the worst meat she could buy, and again she brought a cow's tongue. 'Is the cow's tongue the best and also the worst meat in the market?' he asked her. 'Yes,' the maid replied; and how true it is; it is the best and the worst in every market. It is both in life and death heaven and hell. Control your tongue; do not use it to blaspheme God and slander your neighbour, and always speak well of God and man." He was completely free from slander and libel, and he was more concerned about his own failings than about anyone else's failings, and one cannot say about him as can be said about other fallen beings, 'They can see everyone else's weaknesses, and faults, but can never see their own faults'.

His main concern was for his home, and disliked those who traded in the character of their brothers, and many a sharp arrow he fired at those who got drunk in the blood of the saints; and who are never satisfied unless they can get the head of some John on their plates. While preaching on the text 'If there is anyone who does not have the Spirit of Christ within him, that person does not belong to Him.' "Jesus showed great love towards his fellow beings when on earth; and if His Spirit is within you, you are like Him; if you possess an unforgiving spirit, you are denying the Christ, 'Love can cover a host of sins.' How unlike many who profess Christ, when one looks at how little love they have towards hiding the faults and failings of their brothers; many give the impression that their witness is as big as the field of Naboth, but they never showed as much as a foot's width of love towards burying the weaknesses of their brothers. You are gentle, it is true, with your own; you have your large cemetery for your own use, so that you ran with your pick and shovel;

and after getting someone to show you the grave, you dug up the sins of your brother, causing a stink to the world and the church., and this with so much pleasure as many a one had in digging at a vein of silver and gold out of the earth. As no one would like to see the opening of the grave of a relative' and see the dogs of the neighbourhood carrying the bones here and there in their mouths; this would be enough to raise the blood to your face and draw tears from your eyes; and if your blood is nearly freezing, and if your eyes had dried, they would still trickle. And how do you feel when raising up the bones of very close relatives who are nearer to you than those named, the old sins of your brothers, like a collection of bones in the mouths of corgis - the bloodhounds of hell - and the hypocritical spaniels of the church? If you are not able to blush at seeing the nakedness of your brothers, and do your best to cover them, you are like Noah's son Ham, and likely to receive the same judgement, namely God's curse, because you did not cover your brother's nakedness. God will note your sins at the last day, and you will be paid with your own coins. 'If there is anyone who does not have the Holy Spirit within him, then he has nothing.'

He was of a peaceful nature and not at all quarrelsome. The Rev. James Davies, Rhydargaeau, ministered with him for many long years; from the time James Davies left Arminianism (or as he use to say, until Calvinism came to him) until his death some two years before that of Dafydd Evans. During the time that they held separate views they used to argue often about it. One day in Troedyrhiw there were two tailors working in the house, and a few other men were also there, the majority of whom held

Arminiastic views, and a lively argument ensued with Dafydd Evans arguing against them. During the argument James Davies entered, and the 'men of the needles' realized a battle was looming, and smiled at each other and one of them acting as the 'instigator of a quarrel'. James Davies was told what they were discussing, and that much had been said about the subject. But in spite of all the efforts of the two tailors, they failed to achieve their aim, that was, 'to get the 'two generals' to fight a battle. They could not get the old Calvin to say anything, but merely puffed away quietly at his pipe, and his contribution confined to merely 'yes, yes, no, no'. But after James Davies left the arguing was resumed. "Why didn't you oppose James Davies?", the 'instigator of the quarrel' asked. " O," Dafydd Evans said, "he is older than me, and I do not oppose an old man - I was quite prepared for him to carry the day, but as I am older than all of you, you should listen and give in to me as I gave in to James Davies." There had not been one cross word or disagreement between the two old patriarchs throughout their long ministry.

Although of a generally peaceful nature, yet he did have a quick, uncontrollable temper. He was then as wild as nettles; he slashed the slates into pieces many a time, and even the presence of hundreds of people would stop him from pouring out his feelings, and 'firing many arrows'. He was very much against three things connected with unknown preachers arriving to preach, that of arriving without an invitation -arriving late - and failing to turn up at all. It cannot be said for certain which of these three situations annoyed him the most. A missionary was booked to come to the Ffynnon; the time for him to arrive came; the chapel was full, and those present were eagerly looking forward to his arrival, but there was no sign of him. The service started - hymn singing - prayers - still no sign of him, and it was eventually realized he would not come at all. As the oldest minister present, the Rev. James Davies was asked to preach, but he refused, 'Ask Dafydd Evans to do so' he said. The members persisted with their request, and he also refused to preach.

"Preach! Preach!", the leaders kept on saying. With this he got to his feet, and very annoyed, excitedly said, "No!, no indeed, I will most definitely not preach, because even if Jesus Christ came here today he would not do so; it is the missionary we are expecting. We will hold a prayer meeting and remember to pray for the brother who has disappointed us today, and every other brother, to get the strength never to break a promise."

One Sunday afternoon a preacher arrived without having made a previous arrangement - Dafydd Evans asked him questions in a rather curt manner where he was a minister, and what were his religious beliefs, and said, "No one is allowed to preach here without having been invited." With this he then went into the pulpit and read and prayed in a gripping manner, and was by then in a better mood, and asked the visitor to preach a sermon, but the preacher had by this time taken offence and refused the request. "Don't then", he (Dafydd Evans) said in a voice that everyone could hear, "I have a short sermon, and I will preach as well as you."

Another time a minister who had been invited to preach at Ffynnonhenry was late in arriving, and Dafydd Evans getting rather prickly while waiting read a chapter, and a hymn was sung - still no sign of him; He (D.E), then prayed and still the minister had not arrived. Dafydd Evans was about to become resigned to the fact that the invited minister would not arrive at all, then announced a hymn to be sung: A three verse hymn written by William Williams.

As he was finishing reading the second verse he saw the visiting preacher walking through the chapel door, and shouted, "Well he comes congregation wreathed in smiles, and the visitor, poor thing, could not understand what was taking place. Dafydd Evans also took offence with another preacher, and very quickly put on quite a long face, but then very soon forgave him. He would very often and very quickly cry for forgiveness. It is most unlikely that the sun ever set on his anger, and the whole country was very fond of him in spite of all his faults.

In dealing with people and matters to do with the rules, and teachings of the church, he was always honest and upright. Some of his observations and sayings at times were both jocular and also scornful, and as cutting as a razor. There was a well-known preacher in Carmarthenshire and Cardiganshire at the time; one who violated the Kingdom of Heaven; I will not name him now, but I strongly believe he has by now found the 'nook and reached the shore'. He was asked to participate in Ffynnonhenry, and he was long in coming, but longer still after he had arrived, until the few people in the congregation were 'praying hard' that the sermon would come to an end, and when he had finished Dafydd Evans exploded, and addressing the preacher said, "I don't know who raised you, and who in the name of everything decided that you should become a preacher. Even if God had raised you, he would possibly have made something of you, and if the devil put something in your head, and if people had raised you they'd come and listen to you; but it must be the case that you raised yourself." Such a verbal thrashing, I believe, would have been enough to even stop 'any animal tiring the sheep'.

There was someone named John who was 'sometimes' a member of Ffynnonhenry, but he was very fond of 'John Barleycorn', who would 'go over the top' during the September sales. He attended a 'Preparatory Meeting' in the chapel in July to ask if he could become a member, and Dafydd Evans said, "Well again asking if he could be accepted as a member. Do you have anything against him? Remember John, turning towards him, I have nothing against you, and I believe that no one else has anything against John being accepted. Brothers and sisters, it will only be for a short period he wants to be a member; only until about the 29th of September, and it would be mean of us if we refused to accept him until then." He went on and said to John, "I advise you to wait until the auctions have taken place, and let it also be delayed over the winter months." Before the coming of fairs and other public events in the area he would say to the people. "My dear people! From a moral standpoint, during the next week it will be freezing, and there will be the danger that you will slip and fall; remember to put plenty of 'ice nails under your boots.'"

CHAPTER SIX
SERMONS

One spring night Dafydd Evans had been invited to preach, The text could possibly be from the fifth chapter of Mark, or Luke, chapter 8, and it was about the woman who had bled for twelve years, and who managed to touch the 'hem of Jesus' garment', and as a result was healed. Unfortunately, there is not a verbatim copy of the sermon to be had, but here is the gist of what he said:

"It was an incident that happened when our Blessed Saviour, was on one of the roads to Capernaum. He was going to raise Jairus's daughter from death back to life. We should notice (1) The faith of the woman, (2) The healing she experienced because of her faith, (3) Her condition before she came to Christ, and (4) The lessons from this important miracle for us today.

We notice the faith of the woman, a faith both strong and determined, yet there was a weakness in her that did not prevent her being healed because her weakness gave an opportunity for the strength of the 'Medicine'. She was praised in the end because she not only believed in the 'Word', but that there was virtue even in His dress - that is surely strong faith. She believed He was the Almighty, and she was ready to believe He was omniscient, but that He did He not know immediately who had touched his dress - this is the weakness in her faith. But Jesus did not reproach her for this, but said to her, "Your faith has healed you." Her faith was in one respect weak but in another way it was strong, but her faith was strong in the most important thing for her, namely, her certainty that He had the ability to heal her. This faith has been witnessed in many others beside this woman, for example, Jeroboam, who sent his wife to Ahab the prophet to ask him whether the boy would live. It is a wonderful thing to have faith, that is to believe in God and Christ, that He is Almighty, omniscient and always present. Mary and Martha did not have enough faith that Jesus Christ was almighty, and could raise Lazarus, otherwise they would not have objected to the moving of the stone that sealed his tomb. But in spite of this Lazarus came out alive through the virtue of the 'Word', "Lazarus, come out", and so the power that is in Jesus could be seen in spite of man's weakness.

(2) A rapid healing took place. As soon as she touched the hem of His garment, 'and the woman was whole from that hour', although according to man's opinion. There were many disadvantages against such a thing happening. The disease was an old one - twelve years. Another thing, quacks had made a botched job of it when trying to heal the woman, 'where there is a carcass, there will congregate the eagles.' Where there is a sick person, an old woman especially, plenty of quacks will call. Her condition had been made worse because they had treated her. Another thing, she had become physically weaker, and short of money, having spent all her wealth on doctors, and the condition made worse. "Who touched me?" Jesus asked. Everyone denied

that they had touched Jesus; Jesus turning around noticed the woman who had touched him. He asked again, "Who touched my clothes without permission?" Everyone kept on denying responsibility, boys, girls and women. "Not me," one said "Not me," said another. Jesus said, "Virtue has gone out towards a sick person, and that person has been completely cured.

"Who stole the Medicine?" He asked again. "Not me," a young girl said, "I am well enough," (far too healthy). "I was too far away." said a young boy (too far by a long way; too far away is half the crowd.) But the point is, someone has stolen and the thief must be found. No one has the right to steal the body or the soul of a person without the Saviour knowing. At last a woman came forward and confessed, and she fell at the feet of the Teacher, crying bitterly, and trembling with fright from head to foot, frightened she lost her health again, and that she would be punished for stealing. "Why," shouted a woman, "didn't she confess much sooner, instead of all of us being suspected because of her?" (No one is suspecting you.) "Yes," another said, "why didn't she ask permission before touching the Teacher's dress - the devilish thief." (There is no danger that anyone will ever steal from Jesus.) "Forgive me, friends, I was in the wrong, and I am very sorry that anyone was worried because of what I did," the woman said, "I will confess everything. I had hundreds of pounds twelve years ago when the illness struck me - going to this doctor and another doctor - taking their drugs, and some of them very bitter - pills sometimes, and a bottle at other times, and those as sour as vinegar; persisting in taking them but I was no better, often worse; medicines that healed others made me worse; large bills as long as my arm arriving every day, and I was struggling to pay them, but in the end the money finished, and the 'old doctors' would not call to see me then, but while the money lasted they called every day. I then felt very sad, my condition was getting worse, and I decided that death was the answer. But then I heard about Jesus of Nazareth, that He healed all kinds of diseases and sickness among the people, and I came to believe that He could cure me. But the big question was, how could I meet Him. Someone told me that a gentleman named Jairus had sent for Him because his daughter was ill, and that He was coming through Capernaum at twelve o'clock today. This is the whole truth that I am saying to you, yes, the whole truth. My disease was by now very serious, not suitable for me to come among a crowd of people; that is when it came to me that I would touch the hem of his garment without anyone knowing. It was not without fear that the people would mark me out as they moved forward towards him. I then stretched out my finger very gently on the edge of his blessed dress, without anyone but myself knowing, and without thinking that God in the flesh was so near to me, and except for my disease I have nothing to pay him for my healing." "I do not want a penny," said the Teacher, "I do not heal people for silver or gold. Go in peace, your faith has healed you." The woman said that Jesus had healed her, but Jesus said that it was the woman's faith. Who do we believe? We can believe both; both say the truth. "Your faith healed you."

True virtuous faith belongs to Jesus Christ - from the edge of His clothes - from his spit - from His shadow - from His word - from calling Him beloved, like the woman from Canaan - from the crown of thorns - from the spear that pierced His blessed side, or from the cross from which He hung, or from the grave in which

He lay. "Now," the woman continued, "I am fully recovered, strong, able to work and able to earn my living; I will go home to spin or knit stockings I will pay you, my Lord, in all honesty for healing me, and I will give you a pair of fine white stockings, the best a woman ever knitted as a present for you. O! my kind benefactor." "I never desired silver or gold, or clothes," Jesus said to her, "go in peace, your faith has healed you, be rid of your sickness." And now we will listen to her thankfulness for her valuable healing, in the words of Psalm 103, "Bless the Lord, my soul, with all my being I bless His holy name. Bless the Lord my soul." "She has really given thanks very well, exclaimed a girl in the crowd. "She had every good reason to give thanks," another woman said. Who is there who has not had a good reason to give thanks, but possibly not for the same thing? She is rid of her disease. What better reason could there be; getting rid of a disease that she had suffered from for twelve years, no more than for a man or woman giving thanks who had suffered a disease for fifty-two years? The man who said to the woman, "Be healed of the disease," and said to another "No disease will come near your home" should be given thanks in the same way. It is the same grace that kept that person from suffering worry and pain as for the one who suffers an ailment.

On another occasion his text could be John 3, verse 8, "The wind bloweth where it listeth, and thou hearest the sound thereof, but cannot tell from where it cometh, and whither it goeth; so is everyone who is born of the Spirit."

There follows what Dafydd Evans said in the sermon, "The wind is invisible, unfeeling and slippery. Although God holds it in his hands, and moves and walks on its wings, yet for us it is slippery but we can hear its sound, and see its effect. It blows wherever it wants, I mean the wind of heaven, not machine wind made by man. The wind is one of three able servants that God has created, namely, water, fire and wind. These three are essential to man and animal, they are good servants, cruel, destructive and dreadful masters. It is quite easy to rule them as long as care is taken of the three. The wind is the chief servant - water is the second - and fire is the third, or in other words, the minor servant. The chief servant rules the other two, and they can do nothing about it. They often hear its strong voice giving them orders to do this or that, after feeling its heavy hand beating them, until their sides are creaking, but they are unable to do anything at all about it.

They have never seen it - don't know what it looks like - what its colour is, whether it is black or white, blue or green. It is totally invisible to everyone, this is like its Creator. The chief servant beats severely the servants under it, but sometimes not without a good reason; fair play to the chief servant, only it has gone away from its home, leaving a fleet of ships for the second servant to take them to the continent, but on returning found the second servant sleeping quietly in the sun, and the ships as if they were tickling it to wake up. But here comes the head servant shouting at it to wake up, and beginning tidying it up, and whipping it, and blowing into its eye until it was furious - stirring up and causing the sea to foam wildly, and got hold of its collar in the end and knocked out its brains against the rock of Lochdyn, and many a ship sank while writhing from the scolding it received from the head servant. The second and third servants often quarrel, and it is difficult to know which one is the victor. But it is the second that is the stronger if it uses all its strength, and if it begins early.

The head servant, that is the wind, is master of the minor servant as well; it will not work as well unless it is after it all the time. It drives it wildly ahead, to burn cities and large forests. When the head servant chases the third servant, O! it is dreadful towards the inhabitants of the forest, and cities and dwellings; but if it turns against heather or gorse covered mountains, they hinder it from causing as much damage. However much of a master the head servant is, our Saviour has the measure of it, and he is the only one that can master it. He mastered it long ago when it was in its most deceitful mood, shaking and roaring like a giant; and the Creator only said, "Hush! Be still., and it became as quiet and harmless as a lamb; and how the second servant smiled on seeing the head servant meeting its master for once! The three servants, the wind, the water and fire, can be seen working together for the benefit of man, on land and at sea, in the air.

Another thing; it lacks feeling and is elusive. You can have a can or a bottle of water - you can move fire, but you cannot move the wind of heaven. It is not possible to know where it begins, or what causes it. It is not because of the world turning, because it remains the same at all times, but the wind is not like that. Although no one sees it, or where it comes from, or where it goes, we can hear its sound, and we can see the results of what it can do.

The actions of the Holy Spirit, both in the Old Testament

and the New Testament, can be compared to it, especially in its gracious and beneficial effect on men's souls. It has many servants under it, and it rules 'convinces the world of sin, and the justice of judgement'. It is said that the Lord God made the wind travel over the earth after the flood; and the waters were stilled, and have not been still since. It says in sacred songs that the church prays for the gifts of the Holy Spirit, to have the likeness of the wind, "Come you, north wind, south wind blow over your garden," The works of the Spirit on bones as Ezekiel saw in his vision, are being likened to the wind. The wind had nothing to start its work in the valley except dry bones Samson had an ass's bones, and Adam had a rib to make Eve. But when the wind was called life came to them and they became living beings. Many sinners are seen like the dry bones; so unlike were they to the bones that become living saints. The wind is strong and powerful. Elias tells about the time he was on the mountain; we are to understand that it is the spiritual wind that is meant by "the strong wind of heaven" tearing the mountains and the rocks apart.

On the day of Pentecost the Holy Spirit, through the Word, worked very well; "And suddenly there came from heaven as of a mighty rushing wind, and it filled all the house where they were sitting." (Acts 2:2) At that time they were clothed with a strength from above, all receiving 'waterproofs' and 'firepower' clothes, suitable for standing in the permanent courts of the high priests and Caesar, devils, and prisons, the gallows, and axes, and the strings of death. They were dressed by the Spirit with God's armor, in a military uniform, so that they could fight the lion and the dragon, and to win against them. They could play at the mouth of the home of the snake, and stretch forth their hands into the entrance of its home, and stand in the fire without suffering any harm. They could like David, run through the army without receiving any wounds, and jump high walls without breaking a single bone, and more than anything, the cloth hat, they received from the heavenly, Holy Spirit, was 'death proof.' They could challenge death, the most fearful of kings, and throw in its face "Where is thy sting?", and say, "Where is your victory?", and sing the sweet verses of Paul, "To God be the glory that gives us the victory".

The wind blessed the souls on the day of Pentecost, besides straightening out the Apostles, it worked wonders on the listeners and the preachers. It could clothe the sick, it could strip the leaders of their own sense of importance, and prick them so that it left a mark on them. Not everyone was left to leave as they came. They were not allowed to leave hard hearted, but the wind of Elias - it tore away the mountains, it split the rocks; it made the desert shiver, and it broke the cedars of Lebanon. Many of the priests were moved by the wind to the heavenly port, and it moved some of Caesar's family to the faith that is in the gospels, and left its mark on the whole of mankind. It convinced the world of its sin, of justice and judgement, especially the sin of the unbelievers, the Spirit even turned this evil giant.

"The wind blows where it desires." It cannot be stopped or ruled. The Holy Spirit is a free agent. The Holy Spirit works to free mankind. It cannot be turned or hindered by the power of man or by angels. It blows wherever it wants to, in spite of everyone and everything. Jonah wanted to stop the wind, but the wind forced him to Nineveh; and in the same manner to the house of Cornelius, and Saul of Tarsus who tried to fight against it, but it blew the old persecutor in spite of this; it lifted him completely from himself and his law, until he landed in Christ and His justice. He threw him on his knees to pray: "Heavenly breeze, blow into this meeting."

Or perhaps it would be Jonah's sermon to the people of Nineveh, and in the body of the sermon these observations - God said to Jonah, "I want you to go to Nineveh." "What for?" Jonah asked. "To preach," God said. "I haven't got a sermon," Jonah replied. "O, I will give you a sermon," God said, "In forty days Nineveh will fall!" "No, I will not go, that is all a lie; I know you too well that they will listen to such a sermon," remarked Jonah. "Are you saying that I am a liar? God asked. "Go to Nineveh immediately because I am telling you to do so." "No indeed," Jonah said, "go yourself." "I will make you go." God told him. "I will make certain that you will not." Jonah replied, and off he went as if he was a murderer, down to Joppa, and there decided to go on a ship for Tarsus, and immediately agreed with the captain the cost of the journey, and did not haggle over the price, but paid on the spot, and in he went on board the ship, and the ship set sail. "I'm alright now, I will win this wager with God," Jonah said.

But God sent the 'head servant', namely the wind, like a policeman after him in order to get him to Nineveh. But how could he be got out of the ship? Well, the 'head servant' started blowing, whipping up the water, which jumped up and threatened to swallow the ship and all that was in it. The sailors began to panic; everyone calling on God - truly, they were better than many like those without hope and without God; they were even better than Jonah. But he was sleeping quietly near the ship's side, and they threw out the 'furniture' to see if things would improve, but it would not happen as long as the 'strong piece of 'furniture' (**Jonah) was still in the ship. They cast lots, and it fell on Jonah to give an account regarding himself, and would he confess everything there and then, and it was a strange confession. "How can we still the sea?" the men asked. "Throw me into the sea, Jonah said, and the sea will become still." In truth, and this was his game, he would prefer to drown than go to Nineveh. He would prefer to lose his life before losing his wager with God. But it was difficult for the sailors to decide to give him up to the sea. "Let us try to return to land," they said, as now then, all hands on for a while." But it did not make any difference. The 'head servant' continued to roar like a bear that had lost its cubs - pressing the ship in its arms until it was creaking, and saying in its own language, "Throw that old man into the sea; throw him overboard, otherwise I will drown all of you." In the end he decided to do just this. A priest was called to read the funeral service - let him be buried in a religious way, anyway; and he was gently placed in the sea. Well the 'two servants', wind and water, had got him out of the ship, but how was he to get to Nineveh? Near the ship there was a large whale ready to take him. "Uff!" the whale said and swallowed him without ceremony. as if it was swallowing a drake. But if it did, he soon regretted doing so; Jonah was tough all over. After swallowing Jonah, the old whale dashed away through the ocean, and the fish shouted after him, "Hey!, Hey!, what's the matter with you today?" "O,

I swallowed a man," replied the old whale. "Tut!, Tut! You have swallowed a man many times before, and I am sure you will also enjoy this man." "Yes, yes! I should do and a small one, but the devil is alive in my stomach." "Vomit it out then, vomit it out immediately." "I can't, I just can't." and away it raced through the ocean, knocking into this fish and another fish, and saying, "Oh! This is awful!" Blowing and groaning, and often saying, "This is awful, if I can get rid of this one, I will never again swallow another man." But Jonah was an old, stubborn preacher, failing to understand and not knowing where he was. He felt as if he was between mountains because of the high waves, and lying on a pillow of seaweed, and could not go to sleep as he did when on board the ship, and he was praying with all his heart. The whale wished that he could get rid of Jonah, and after three days and three nights he found relief, and threw the old preacher in a lump on to the beach. Jonah jumped on his feet and shouted, "Goodbye to you, good riddance to you," "Good riddance to you too," replied the whale, and how grateful was Jonah to have escaped from the whale, but the fish was equally as grateful to have been rid of Jonah.

And God said to Jonah, for what was the second time, "And now you will go Nineveh." He did not give an answer, and away he went very quietly. Ah! That shook you, you lost your wager Jonah; there is nothing for you to do now but preach. In the city he, for the first time started preaching, and shouting as loud as he possibly could said, "Another forty days and Nineveh will fall" and he then proceeded through the city, with a strange unearthly look on his face, shouting, "In forty days Nineveh will fall." Children and old people gathered around him in their hundreds, and followed him along the streets. Many others stood at the corner of a street, and, and one of them shouted, "Hey Jack, that is the one we threw into the sea between Joppa and Tarsus. "Yes," don't you remember me telling you that I believed he had been swallowed by a whale? There was something odd about the old man." "Yes, as I am standing here, I am certain a whale did swallow him. Look, he is covered with the fish scales of a herring; but like us the whale did not get any peace until it got rid of it." Onwards Jonah went on through the streets without talking to anyone; his face with a frozen frown like the Sinai, shouting, "In forty days Nineveh will fall." The people began to repent, realizing their danger. He then stood in front of a cobbler's shop, still shouting, "Another forty days and Nineveh will fall." O! boys, boys," said the cobbler, "God's prophet has arrived; judgement has come to us. Let us repent; if God sees fit to forgive us, I will never again use the bark of the alder tree instead of leather." Away went Jonah and stood in front of a grocer's shop, and crying out, Forty days and Nineveh will fall," "O! boys, boys," the grocer said, Judgement has come to us; we have been very wicked; this is only what we deserve, but if the Lord will be prepared to forgive us this time, we will be better, we will not give goods that are under weight, or put sand in the sugar ever again." Jonah then stood in front of a large draper's shop, going through his sermon in a frightening manner, "In forty days," "O!" the shopkeeper said, "here is the God of Israel's prophet telling us of a dreadful judgement on us soon. We are finished. Let us repent, repent; it is possible, boys, that our tears will save us, go and search for every canvas sack in the shop so that we can repent, and if it is His will, save us this time;

we will never give false measures, nor deceive on the price, or cheat on the trimmings ever again." On Jonah went, and stood in front of a large building, where there were a number of girls staring at him through the windows and others standing near the doors. It was a large brothel, "Forty days again, and Nineveh will fall." "Girls, girls," someone who was standing nearby said, "it is all over for your trade; you have been too wicked, and your wickedness has brought judgement on the city." "Mind your own business," an impudent girl shouted, we have as much chance of inheriting eternal life as you have." Jonah continues his walk through the city, and went to the King's palace, and stood in front of His Majesty as if he would have stood in front of a beggar. With stick in hand, and eyes blazing, and the voice one of doom and destruction, "Forty days again, and Nineveh will fall." he shouted, and the king came down at once from his throne, discarded his crown, threw down his sceptre, and took off his royal robes, and put on sackcloth, so that the whole city would do the same. "The people of Nineveh believe in God, and a period of fasting will be announced, and from the smallest to the greatest will all wear sackcloth." And God saw their acts, that they were turning away from their wickedness, and God forgave them, and was sorry for what he had said he would do to Nineveh. This offended Jonah, and he went out of the city, and watching it from a short distance started to severely scold God. "Here we are," he said, I am now in a pickle; you sent me here to tell them a lie, they will surely kill me, and it will be no wonder. I had a feeling that this is how it would turn out. I said before leaving home that you would not do what you said you would; I knew that if they showed the slightest sign of repentance you would be the first to forgive them, and withhold judgement, because that is what kind of 'old flannel' you are. You prefer foreigners to me. I am really offended that you sent me here to tell them a lie, and in the end be killed by a pack of thieves. I am sorry I did not drown in the sea. O! that I could die now."

Many on hearing stories about Dafydd Evans could get the impression that what he said was both flippant and of little consequence; but they could not have made a bigger mistake. All his sermons were Biblically based, and contained the cream of Christianity - full of invitations and warnings to the irreligious, and giving comfort and help to the saints. His texts were usually carefully chosen, and without doubt better in content than arranged. His 'army' would not always be neatly arranged, but at all times lively and brave, and would range far and wide in his attacks, which were daring and unflinching towards the enemy. He had not learnt to fight with a sword and spear, but with a bow and arrow or some other implements that became his weapons - the mattock, or shovel, or possibly an axe, if they could floor the enemy, and this was his main subject and aim. His weapons were purposeful and up to the work that had to be done.

His sermons were a mixture of doctrine and the practical - from the pictorial to the suggestive - inducing 'the wicked to leave their way of life and return to the Lord - and for the saints to strive towards perfection - working faithfully and quickly in the vineyard - to battle bravely in the field of battle until total victory is achieved.' The cross was his central point and his home, and in his lively and irregular travels, he would never go so far as to lose sight of Calvary; and his imagination behaved like a prancing pony not used to the reins, and escaped from the rider, but he would catch it as easy as clutching a clump of growth from Golgotha; and worked steadily enough to 'harvest the gold', and the 'expensive pearls' for those fallen from grace. He is no more romantic or wild in any of his sermons, as he was in his sermon on Jonah.

CHAPTER 7
SPIRITUALLY NATURAL

Dafydd Evans was a very popular socializer; as popular in one place as any other - in a house or out in the open; and king of the hearth; and when he spoke everyone was in a good mood, from the four year old to the patriarchal grandfather in his favourite armchair; and it could be said that even the cat and dog would be amused by his descriptions and wit. As he left the chapel, a crowd would follow him, and he, stick in hand, stopping every other step, making an amusing remark about something that happened in the past, or was to come, or was happening at the time. It could be a crow, bird, or a sheep, or cows, or the mountain would be giving rise to his comment; and his observations were so natural, lively, easy to understand, and amusing that the 'disciples of the loaves' were often in a good mood.

It could be that his subject was one of the parables of Jesus; the evil spirits entering the swine. "It must have been a remarkable sight, wasn't it boys? Yes indeed, yes indeed; seeing a multitude of pigs, and those full of evil spirits running into the sea! O they were really moving! This idea is natural to the devil; he was the first to think of 'marking a pig', and no one has marked it afterwards. A legion of devils in a multitude of pigs! How many were there? Two thousand possibly. A legion of six thousand? Hold on, how many were in each pig? Three, Possibly? Yes indeed, three in every pig, one on its back, one forward, and one in the middle, the front one holding the ears, the one at the back holding the tail, and the ears and tails of the Gadarene pigs red ever since then. Talk about running! It is better with the devil to make as much mischief as he can even if it is not as much as he would like to do. If he could not put souls in hell, he would make certain that he could enter the pigs rather than be idle. If he lost his present work and was to become a pig-drover - he would make a famous one. O they were moving very fast! But it was the poor pigs only that drowned. The old devils were able to swim like ducks." It is possible that these observations of his were later made during a sermon on a Sunday, and when preaching that Sunday, it is possible that he would not be able to leave out any of what he had originally said while walking on the road.

When he had been invited to preach at some other chapel, there was great excitement among members of the family where he would be staying the night; the servant and the maid, the master and mistress, and the children from the youngest to the oldest walking around with broad smiles on their faces. "Dafydd Evans, Ffynnonhenry is here next Sunday;" and they would be very excited at the thought of welcoming him. It was around May Day, and it happened to be quite cold; and he could be seen coming, riding his horse, and the men-folk of the house running to meet him. "How are you today, Mr. Evans?" "Not very well, I fell off this horse the day before yesterday; and if horses go to hell, this one is certain to go there; because he is an extremely wicked one." The maid, her face wreathed in smiles, ran into the house to tell her mistress that Dafydd Evans had arrived; and by this time the sound of his footsteps on the path outside could be heard, and his voice also heard by those in the house, and all inside the house very excited. "You have arrived then, Dafydd Evans?" the lady of the house said to him. "You decide, my dear Mrs. Jones, but it seems I have. O yes, I am the one, it is easy for you to recognise me, you have only to see me once, because I am rather ugly." "Sit! Dafydd Evans'. It can be said that even the ugliest thinks a great deal of himself, as much as the most handsome person in the land, and I never saw even the smallest who did not think a great deal of himself. O no indeed - I once saw a four and a half foot tall man showing authority as much as a great emperor, say, 'Silence here; no more noise,' and his wife was big enough to put one like him under each arm and throw them over the hedge, but then small persons should be careful that the same thing does not happen to them that once happened to a gnat on going to London to visit the Queen. It decided to go to London on a very hot summer's day by coach, but it was too full for him to get a seat. "Well," he said to himself "I'll have to wait until tomorrow, but I may be able to get on a seat outside the coach today after all," and away he went, full of his own importance. "Strange," he said as the horses galloped along, "It is surprising the amount of dust raised from the road today!" On arriving in London he decided to go and tidy himself up before going to see Her Majesty, and went into the garden of Buckingham Palace to do this - and after washing and shaving, and much preparation , and looking into the mirror to see that he looked alright, said proudly to himself, "I believe I look alright now." "Hello," a wren asked, "who is there?" "It is I" answered the gnat in a pompous voice, "I am going to see Her Majesty." "I will soon put an end to your pleasure," the wren said, and at that effortlessly swallowed the gnat, and that is often the end of such pompous beings." "Sit! Dafydd Evans, come towards the fire." "Yes, that is the best thing to do, my dear Mrs. Jones, and a fire is very welcoming today; my goodness sometimes a fire is needed at this time of the year. It was cold coming over that moor. March and April can, with their cold hands, bring hailstones even on May's gentle skin. Dear me, it is cold! Far too cold for the cuckoo to sing, it has become hoarse since yesterday morning. And do you know what the villain is doing at the present moment? Looking for other birds' nests, stealing the eggs so that she can lay her eggs in the nest."

After supper, followed by reading and prayers, the conversation restarted. Most of what he had to say were reminiscences. If someone too eager and not very intelligent had tried to stimulate him to say more, he would probably become quiet and stubborn, like a donkey, and would throw him into the gutter. As he spoke his listeners kept on hoping for more; the man sat on one side of the fire, and his wife on the other side, and the children would have been allowed to stay down longer than usual that night - the most important of the servants, and the next in line sitting there, as well as Johnny, the youngest servant lurking behind the door and the maids listening intently from the kitchen, and finding the excuse to attend to the fire more than necessary;

He spoke with as much enthusiasm on the hearth or on the road to one or two as he would to two or three hundred in a chapel. The blacksmith working on his anvil listening to him would make many a mistake when dealing with the iron and similarly the tailor would make many a wrong stitch, and even stab his own finger while trying to better understand what he was hearing. More often than not it was in the houses of Sion, where people searching for the eternal crowns, sat at his feet. He would often relate his most important sermons on the hearth of farms in the district, with three or four 'congenial spirits' holding up his arms; and especially one very amusing occasion. Johnny (the Inviter) was standing at the door of a farm in the area and was waiting for a long time for entry, with his hat in his hand, his patience wearing thin and shouting by this time rather unseemly remarks. He had simply come to invite the residents of the house to a feast, and was kept waiting while the minister finished what he had to say. But who was talking but Dafydd Evans inviting them to a heavenly 'feast' and two tailors sitting cross-legged on the table and also a mason present, and the people who lived in the house, sitting around the fire, and the 'Inviter' soon ended up an ardent listener, completely forgetting his own chatter and the reason for calling at the house.

A person said that he (Dafydd Evans) once took his pony down to the smithy, and wanted the pony's shoes to be removed and new shoes put on in their place. He said, "Sam, you make two shoes and I will make the other two." And so it was done, but at the same time he did not stop talking for a second. "Do you know anything about Moses, Sam?" "Yes, Dafydd Evans," Sam replied. "He died didn't he?" "Do you know where he was buried?" "No, I don't," replied Sam, "and I don't suppose you know either." "No I don't, and the devil doesn't know either,"

Dafydd Evans admitted. He continued, "He had seen many very important people die in Israel, and it is certain that he attended every one of the funerals as well. He never missed a funeral of one of the important people in Israel. But he was not warned of Moses' funeral. He had given much thought as to when Moses would die, and had every intention of attending his funeral, and had very carefully marked a grave for him. But when he found out that Moses had died without him knowing, look out! There he was swearing and tearing out his hair, and he was in a terrible temper. He was jumping up and down- nearly as high as the stars! If he could only find out where the grave was situated he would ruin a whole nation in spite of God. They would be worshipping there still today. But the old devil did not discover the grave's location; and he will not find out until the day that Moses rises from the grave; but it will be too late for him by then, and how annoyed he will be that he won't know the spot." "Do you know, Sam, who the greatest fool was that has ever been when it comes to making a bargain? It was hairy Esau; selling his birthright for a mere bowl of broth! Such a price to pay for such a trifling meal that would hardly satisfy his stomach. If the fool had only held out longer when bargaining, he could have had a cauldron full of broth, more than enough to satisfy him." With all this talk, Sam found himself making four shoes, almost without knowing it.

If he had no one to talk to then he would find as much pleasure in his own company as he would in the company of hundreds. Some men left on their own are the most miserable 'flowers' imaginable. They are sharp-tongued about others but have nothing to say about themselves. Although Dafydd Evans was extremely fond of the company of others, and society was very fond of him, yet he liked his own company, God, and nature; the problem he faced was to find time to himself, someone would continually be calling in the village where he lived, to see him. Many had travelled miles to the insignificant village of Cynwyl in order to share an hour or two with the very original and witty old preacher. It is an unique quality of talented people of all ages and country, that people had a tendency to treat them as personal property. The Baptists, Independents, Methodists and Anglicans took their utensils to fetch water from Dafydd's well, and there was no difference between them. He was not known as the Rev. Dafydd Evans, the Baptist Minister, but as Dafydd Evans, Ffynnonhenry. Owned by everyone.

Not a man of party, man of fellow beings,
Friend of sinners, and brother of angels
Faithful servant of God, royal priest,
Citizen of the world, a member of Creation.

CHAPTER 8
PRAYERS

Dafydd Evans was famous for his unusual prayers. However famous as a preacher and unusual he was there is no doubt that he was even more so as a supplicant; his prayers were considered to be gripping before he set out as a preacher. Christmas Evans was eager to give a purposeful prayer before he started preaching his sermon; and in the Assembly (Gymanfa) held at Penrhiwgoch in the county of Carmarthen he was due to preach at 10 o'clock, and asked the minister, "get someone who is good at praying to start the service." "Who shall I ask, Mr. Evans?" asked the minister. "Try the boy from Ffynnonhenry," replied Christmas, and this is what he did, and he prayed in a most unusual, easy and gripping manner. When he finished Christmas greeted him by saying to him, "Your prayer pleased me very much my boy." "I was not praying to please you Mr. Evans, but to please God," Dafydd Evans replied. This shows that he had begun his ministry in the proper place, and trading in the only treasure house that supplies souls with 'a better and permanent wealth', and attending the only place where he would have the strength to bravely stand on the battlefield for many years. So different to everyone I had heard previously, he prayed with his eyes wide open, staring at one spot in the chapel. He did not look at any person, but on some unseen being, He was as if he was looking, eyes open, at the Most High God, and he printed on everyone's mind that he was in God's company, and really speaking to the Almighty, on behalf of himself, the congregation and the whole world. He was far above anyone I had heard, and his natural delivery was most beautiful and charming. This is also the opinion of many people who had had the privilege, and had heard him more than I had. A Methodist minister said that he had heard him in a monthly meeting held in Cynwyl, and that he was best there; that he was unusually effective and gripping. He did not speak to God as if he had any doubt of His existence, or as if he was far from him, but as if He was at his side - nearer to him than anyone else who was around him - as if he saw Him, realizing his loving and gracious presence. I would find it difficult and unusual to have this feeling when I attempt to pray, or when listening to others praying; but did feel that way when seeing and listening to Dafydd Evans praying. It is certain that he saw someone else in front of his eyes, and that there was a struggle as there was with Jacob and the angel. His prayers were not a worthless exercise, with no meaning, and clumsy and formal, but an honest striving, difficult, successful cry for God's blessing, and it gave him pleasure to go to the 'throne of grace' in His company.

When visiting another country it is an advantage to have the company of someone who knows the way well - who understands the language - able to talk to the inhabitants - friendly with, and known to the President - having a great interest in the country. It was a pleasure to go with the old patriarch from Ffynnon to the throne of God; he was familiar with the way - knew the language of the country - familiar with the privileges that come from the throne, and having such an interest in the court, so there was not much to ask before receiving. Servants knew him as a special friend of their master, so that one of them would immediately run to fetch some 'manna', or a drop of the 'living water' for him. His knock on the door of the sanctuary was recognized, so that it would not take long before it was opened.

It would give me great pleasure if I was able to present the reader with some of the old pitchers that Dafydd Evans used to draw water from the wells of salvation, and the bells that rang out near the gate of heaven for the spiritual gifts that save; but I have to be satisfied with the imperfect examples that follow. In Penybont, Llandysul, when burying a member of the chapel who had been ill for twenty-six years. He prayed as follows:-

Thank you, Almighty Lord, for giving us the strength to come here today. We have read in your Word of funerals being stopped on the way. Thank you that we have not had to throw the body of our brother to the side of the hedge, and run homewards. But here we are, with your help, here today. We have come because we want to worship you. We are obliged to worship you in every situation, but we could not do it without your help. Give us your help! O, give us your help! It is a sad occurrence that has brought us together; let us feel as we should. Bless all of us as a crowd. You have been balm to give relief to all our wounds, let us accept it. Your treasures will never diminish even after you have satisfied all of us. Bless this church of which our brother was a member. Bless both minister and congregation. Great Lord, bless the relatives who mourn here today, especially the widow and the children. There is here a widow who lost her husband and children who have lost a father. Bless the children who are here and also the ones who are not present. (There were two in America) Some of them on the other side of the ocean. The news has not reached them yet, but it is on its way. Great Lord, prepare their minds to accept the sad and unpleasant news of the death of their father. Keep your promise to those who are on this side of the ocean and those on the others side, you are able to be on both sides of the ocean, we can only be on one side, and we are not much good on one side, but you are on both sides of the ocean, and even on it as well. Be a father to the bereaved - remember this widow; O Lord, it is a dark day for her today - a black, dark day - a cloudy, foggy day - the day of burying her husband. This day for her is pitch black, Lord, keep and lighten her mind. Let her see you on this occasion. Give her the ability to see your face; or let her see your back as did Moses long ago; and if she sees your back she will never have seen a broader back with so many orphaned children and widowed women on it. Let her see your back anyway. She was pleased with her husband. She attended to him with kindness during his illness. She used to lean a great deal on him, although she could not have had much benefit from him for years, yet he was there, and she does not now have any hope of seeing him again on earth. Let her lean on you, and feel your eternal arms supporting her, and the Judge of widows standing on her behalf. Stay with her on her journey through the desert. Be a cloud column before her by day, and a fire at night, and let her, and her children and all of us be taken to the same country as is our hope that her husband has entered. This we freely ask for Jesus' sake. Amen.

Another time he gave thanks in his prayer for freedom:- Thank you, Lord, that axes are used in our day to cut down trees instead of men's heads for following Christ, yes, yes, the heads of far better people than us were cut off for doing what we have the privilege of doing. Thank you, great Lord, for freedom. Amen.

On another occasion he said these words while praying.: Here we have come, O Lord, once again to your house of prayer. The purpose now is to ask for favours from You - asking from one who owns plenty of the things we need - and we are asking one who is always ready to give. Blessed! Yes, forever blessed! You give new feathers to the birds every year and a new beak in turn to the eagle; give each one of us a new head, and you will be praised for ever and ever.

He was more often than not short, gripping and purposeful; and asked and thanked for something special. The congregation felt that he had a message, and wanted everyone to be purposeful in prayer. In one meeting a 'brother' read out a hymn to sing that was not in the least bit striking; rather sharply Dafydd Evans said, "William, what is this old verse you are announcing? Give out a more lively word than that." I'll never tire however long the journey, as long as heavenly grace, William read. "Well said, well said, that is something big," Dafydd Evans said, "William, come and pray again, and pass on your message. If someone approached a gentleman with a message and began by saying, 'Good morning to you sir; it is a fine day; I knew your father and grandfather, they were nice people; you are very rich, you have a fine estate,' the gentleman would more than likely stop him from continuing and say, 'I know that my father and grandfather were

nice people, and that I am rich, but, man, what is your message?'
Come and pray William and give your message in a direct way."
He was always against long and purposeless prayers. He used to
say, "If you get tired of a long-winded prayer, put your head in
water like Peter, and the prayer will soon be shortened, Lord,
keep us!"

He believed in the power and effectiveness of prayer as an answer
to special situations such as praying for the sick, and steadfastly
believed that his prayers for the sick and those in trouble had
been listened to, and answered. He would often pray with
intensity and spoke in a friendly manner, and at times in a very
determined way to the Lord about various things. He could be
heard sometimes talking to God as if he was talking to a friend
who was present and visible. As already mentioned, the Rev.
James Davies was in a ministerial partnership with him for many
years, and during periods of failure and black days for religion in
the Ffynnon, Dafydd Evans would be very upset and depressed.

One Sunday morning while on his way to Ffynnon, he was seen
going into a wood, and as he was there for a long time one or
two members went to look for and to listen to him to see what
was going on and there he was, leaning with his back against a
large oak tree, talking as much as possible with the Lord, and the
following was heard, "Lord," he said "what is the reason for this
lack of success in Ffynnon? What is the reason for it? I want to
know today; I will not move from here until I do find out. No,
no, I cannot show my face like this. If it is my fault, Lord, kill me
at the foot of this tree. If I am the reason for the lack of success

in this great cause, you should kill me out of the way. Yes, kill me, Lord! But if the fault lies with James Davies, do what you like with him, Lord." And if what is said above is fact then a great success 'through the effort in the word' did take place because many people came to ask the way to Sion. It is only the Almighty knows how many showers of blessings passed - how many judgements were prevented, and how many floods of blessings flowed over the country, as a result of the rule of Abraham on the plains, or the vigorous and faithful efforts of Dafydd Evans, Ffynnonhenry, in some wood or other.

As a preacher and minister he was unusually successful - in lecturing, in prayer meetings, in the fellowship that was in the Sunday School. In all aspects, the people found satisfaction and very often found even more. In that age, and to a great extent today, the 'Gymanfa Bwnc', a gathering together for the purpose of questioning members of different Sunday Schools on a passage from the Bible, and was (and to a certain extent still takes place in certain areas today) very popular and beneficial; and it is due to such meetings that the scriptural knowledge of the elderly and middle-aged was so good; and I doubt whether those who were brought up going to Sunday School, and did not take part in such an event as 'Gymanfa Bwnc' with its sessions of question and answer, can compete in the subjects with those who did attend such an event.

But not every good preacher is good at questioning members of a Sunday School on biblical chapters. Dafydd Evans excelled at this. Many remember him in a meeting at Hermon asking questions on a chapter that contains an account of Christ riding towards Jerusalem, and in the middle of his questioning suddenly asked a class of boys, "Hold it, boys," he said, "was it an old or a young ass Jesus was riding?" One boy said, "An old one." Another said, "Fairly old." "Well, truly," Dafydd Evans said, "if it was an old one, the children on that road were better behaved than the children around Hermon and Cynwyl, otherwise they would have injured it - it is said that no one had ever sat on the ass before."

The memory is still fresh with both old men and women of a 'Thanksgiving Meeting' for the harvest in Ffynnon, when it had been so wet at harvest time that nearly all the wheat had rotted in the field, and quite difficult that there would be a spirit of giving thanks; it was a spirit of complaining that ruled throughout the chapel. Dafydd Evans got up on his feet to address the members and said, "I don't know what to say; this service someone said is called a 'Thanksgiving Service' but it is more like a service of complaints. Let us consider the matter for a minute, yes, how bad it has been, but yet it has been worse for many others. We don't have to eat our children or eat each other. Let us think about what we deserve. Not according to our sins. We should take into account God's goodness towards us over the years, and especially His grace! What is one wet harvest compared to tens of dry and seasonal years? We should thank Him more this year than ever before. Having experienced only the tip of His stick we should give thanks that we did not experience its middle or its thickness. Having only been struck by His open hand, we should give thanks that we did not have to feel the effect of His large fist.

He would enlarge on the above and such like, until the congregation would be filled with a sense of submission to what they had heard and thank God for his talent; and this example is only one instance in fifty years of ministry.

Dafydd Evans was a deeply religious man. There are two opinions regarding his godliness by anyone who knew him; and those most familiar with him would be the loudest in telling about his virtues and his responsible nature. This was the unanimous opinion of the public, that he was a godly man - exceptionally godly and the most shiny and priceless gem in every crown. His godliness was not formal, selfish, authoritarian, one-sided and negative, which is so popular in our days, but his was a pure undefiled religion of God and Father, that not only keeps its owner spotless from worldly matters, but lead to 'seeing to the orphans and widows in their adversity'. This wisdom that first of all is pure, then peaceful, gentlemanly, easy to treat, full of mercy, fruitful, limitless and not hypocritical. This was the godliness Dafydd Evans possessed to such a great extent. He required more grace than the ordinary person because he was a man with a perfect nature. Nature had been generous in its gifts, and had endowed him with a generous and lively humanity, and with strong gifts. He was not a man made of wood or stone, but he was lively, a man like lightning, and a man that grace had given him 'telegraphic wires' of feelings and affection to carry gifts between man's heart and God's heart. He was a man who was easy to know which way he was facing; heaven or hell. There are all kinds of men and it is nearly impossible to know how they sail; if I did not know otherwise, they can be in heaven for years.

They are not one iota better or worse than they were since we can remember. Thus they are somehow colourless. But as for Dafydd Evans, he was exciting, passionate, and of an extreme nature; he could have been a famous swearer if grace had not stopped him, and used him for much better work. He did lose the occasional battle. The lava would boil over occasionally in a wild temper, like Etna; but he did not destroy the fields and the orchards at its foot and on its slopes, but he would make the 'living, running water' extinguish it, and mercy winning, and he able to shout out,

"Through the grace of God, I am as I am."

Those who have five talents and those with both talents and other gifts require more strength and grace than those satisfied with less. It takes a great deal more strength to rule the sea than to rule a lake, and it is easier to control an ass than a horse or wild, fiery lightning. It was necessary to floor the 'persecutor' and take him a blind prisoner to God's Kingdom, while Timothy inherited it when only a boy, and was brought into the 'net' naturally. In a thundery shower the small, thin, thin man, weaves his way through the drops, and reaches the house dry, while his companion, ten or twelve times his weight is wet to the skin. "It is through oppression one has to go to enter the life." But we tend to believe that many have entered in between them, whatever, that is the hope. We tend to believe that many have succeeded to have entered, that is our hope. I repeat, it is one thing to find water for sailing a fishing boat, but it is another thing to find enough water for to enable a 'Man of War' to sail.

Thousands would not know of the effort and conquest of the body of death, the powerful wars of the 'laws' and the plentiful supply of grace, if Paul had not written of his experience. We would not know for certain of the depths of the seas of salvation, if we had not seen the occasional Leviathan, such as Manasseh and Saul of Tarsus, swimming in its glistening depths, and we would not know much about the width, height and riches of the merciful Lord, if it wasn't for someone like David, and Columbus finding its fruitful continent, and trading its precious riches.

Dafydd Evans' supply and demands were greater than the ordinary; his vivacity and experiences demanding so much heavenly grace in a week that would be enough for many forever, but he realized to an extraordinary degree the pleasant promise, "Sufficient for you my grace, my strength is made perfect in weakness." In his case grace had an opportunity to stand out in a special way; rarely did anyone give more rope to his passion and tenderness in a more natural way, and yet grace controlled them to a great and admirable extent from transgressing the rules of the spirit, and breaking into the fields and corn fields and preserve the soul. It is one thing to imprison a wild stallion by a rope in the stable, but it is another thing to control its proud walk, its lively frolics and its lightning speed and its remarkable strength, to take its knight from one place to another, or gallop to the field of battle, and smell war from afar. I will say that it is one thing to restrict the natural abilities of the mind, and to fetter natural vivacious passion of the compositions through fasting and unchristian stoicism, but it is another thing to develop in another beauty of character, and to sanctify and be enslaved to the service of God. This to a great extent grace did to Dafydd Evans.

I have been disappointed in a number of my contemporaries I knew so well at one time, like some who were promising human beings, and had a lively nature; I heard that through grace they had been changed, and had taken up preaching the gospel of the Son of God; and our expectations of something of value were high, because grace, I thought at the time, would succeed to work on them. We were on occasions thrown together, and expected them to have changed for the better, but in this we were disappointed. With difficulty we recognized them - the old lives - the vivacity - the open faces - the pleasant smile - the lively expression and the paradisean innocence that were greatly admired were more or less completely lost, and instead the lively, affectionate, healthy, saintly, happy and innocent company that we shared before, we now saw beside us were still the clumsy, unhealthy, sad, unnatural, suspicious, sly person, giving an occasional deep sigh, like a despairing wing, making us say, "Well, if this is the religion of Jesus Christ, we would prefer to be without it." But the Dafydd Evans, Troedyrhiw, was not lost in Dafydd Evans, Ffynnonhenry, but were so alike to each other that their names were often mixed.

A beautiful and gracious development of the last was in truth the foremost of the last. Saul of Tarsus was Paul the Apostle, and the last looked exactly like the first - the eye still as fiery, the look still as keen, threatening and determined, resulting in the saints frightened of him for a long time. They did not know what he was capable of doing, he was much like his own self from a human standpoint, which made them wary of him, as like himself that he could still be the persecutor as he was before. Grace kept the human side of Dafydd Evans careful and complete; nothing went missing. The man was not lost as a Christian, nor the Christian as a man and preacher, but all three were seen in perfect mission, natural and advantageous one to the other. The man shone out in his Christianity, and the Christianity through the preacher and the man. He liked fishing and shooting, and innocent fun as much as he was fond of nature; the only difference was that he did it all as a Christian and a man in truth fearful of God, and whether in the home or outside , in the chapel, or at the riverside, in the fair or the market place, or in a feast or a wedding, everyone felt they were in touch with a man who had his soul at the centre point of goodness, drawing others in the same direction.

It could with a 'glimpse and attempts', that the devil would have been happy to get him (D.E.) to promote him, and to be a general of his army. Many attempts were made on him to change sides, but he stubbornly and bravely refused, and went in the end from strength to strength. He lived a godly life in the world. There are some who live as if they live a godly life 'out of the world' out of society. If they come near to people they flee from them. They are shy with their own kind. They do not run a fair race, and hope that they will be 'crowned'; but Dafydd Evans tried to 'win fairly', and he had been taught to live soberly, righteously and godly in the world of the present time.

He ran towards man, and not away from him, and was praiseworthy and a 'friend of sinners,' and the prayers of Christ were realized to a large extent in him. "I am not praying for you to take them out of the world, but rather that you keep them from the wicked." His religion was tried and tested in the furnaces of calamities and trials, and was successful to withstand the trials. He was like Job, and what it was to be thrown from riches to comparative poverty, and what it was to go from the chapel to prison, and away from his loving family to mix with criminals; yet he remained near to God, and was able to say after it all "The Lord gave, and the Lord taketh away; blessed be the name of the Lord." He came out like gold that had been purified in the fire, more valuable and acceptable than ever before.

His Christian virtues were numerous and brilliant. Although he was quick tempered like Peter, and stubborn like Jonah, yet he was patient in adversity and persevering in prayer, and lived very near to his Lord, and it is interesting to note how he 'drew water from the well of salvation' while in Carmarthen prison, and turning to the old storehouse of the Word for strength to withstand difficulty and the 'wine of comfort to cheer his soul', as can be seen from his diary:-

February 21st 1845, before dawn, had a strange vision from heaven that gave peace to my soul, and there I was in bed in prison. The children of Israel on the sea shore had nothing sweeter or more often.

As I meditated on Romans 15, verse 4, "For whatsoever things were written aforetime, were written for our learning, that we through patience and the comfort of the scriptures have hope."

> *'The darkness of the night will pass,*
> *The clouds of heaven flee,*
> *There'll come the promise true*
> *With pure words will cease.*
> *Then be seen, be seen the promised land*
> *And very soon a shining light.'*

So natural was that hymn in prison, and how it rhymed with the situation at the time! On the 10th of August, the morning of the Sabbath Communion in Ffynnon, and on my own trying to pray for the cause, I found an unspeakable comfort for my troubled soul; I felt that the happiness David had long ago when dancing before the Ark was no greater or bigger; it was the same feeling. Blessed! Thanks for the present time!

I felt great comfort on the 24th of July 1846, when I felt very low in spirit because of my frequent sinning, but God had lifted me up through my reading Psalm 46; especially the 16th verse. Thanks be to God for His regular visits to me. Thanks also for Psalm 116, I will remember this for as long as I live in his world. Amen. So sweet was my poor soul, "Lord, comfort and strengthen me for my lack of faith." This beast has slapped down the greatest saints in every age, like Sara, Moses, Zechariah, the disciples of Jesus before and after the resurrection, Martha,

Thomas and others. They did not believe the Word was true, and that they had seen their dear Lord. To convince them of their error, Jesus ate in front of them, when He did not really want food, and for them to touch His eternal body following His resurrection. It is a serious sin; it is next to blasphemy against the Holy Spirit; it is man's sin, and not the sin of the devil. The last (the devil) does believe. Jesus did not reproach the disciples after His resurrection for their unbelief - "Unbelief leave me alone."

The above quotations from his diary, as well as others quoted previously, are sad, but interesting, and speak volumes about the fountain of his comfort and the sincerity of his character. Whatever feelings and weaknesses they show, hypocrisy and deceitfulness did not touch his life. The quotations do not smell of hypocrisy, nor smell of deceit; but are in the language of honesty and truthfulness, and make us look at their author as a man with a great deal to do with heaven, in truth, and contrast favorably with the man in appearance, and in his words, "a pig with cloven hoof, but not chewing its cud; or like a hare, chewing its cud but not cloven hoof."

"Every person is entitled to his opinion, and every judgement its word," I would rather a thousand times have correctness and honesty in the middle of a desert, than a fair face in a black heart - the face of a Christian and the heart of the devil - outwardly fine and promising, but due to faults in the character a Judas, thief and adulterer, or betraying the Lord, or 'Alexander making big mistakes', or with one hand raised towards heaven in prayer, and the other stabbing the heart of his brother! Dafydd Evans was so very different to this. Yes, I said that our idea about many of the saints of latter days, those whose religiosity was false, crafty and selfish, and who were proud to trick the nations, and endeavored to show up as many faults of their contemporaries as they could, and to praise them as little as possible - they played down their own sins as much as possible, and keep them from being seen by society as much as possible. But Dafydd Evans' character was true and thorough, and to be in his company was good for both body and soul, and the friendship was agreeable and helpful. We felt that we were in the company of a true Christian friend, and the heir of the crown of life - one who did good for his fellow men as soon and as much as possible.

He spoke and practiced a religion that was near to God, and very careful of its existence rather than the hurtful things that were around, and considered that 'life was greater than food, and the body more than clothes.' One felt when looking at his movements that his feet and hands, and tongue did not apishly imitate Christ, but that 'Christ's spirit dwelt in him' and impelled him in a natural way.

He often prayed with the sick, comforted the weak and sorrowful; and rebuked the proud and selfish, and he possessed a lively character, and was very sensitive, and he cried with those who cried and was joyful with those who were happy. He advised everyone, he would rebuke the unruly like a father, and was 'as tender as a mother with her young.' "He took the sheep to his breast, and cherished the lambs," and he was very careful when dealing with children making sure not to hurt them, 'the candles of the Lord's eye.'

His personality, his company and his ministry was destructive to all hypocrisy and deceitfulness, and all kinds of humbug; but constructive to correctness, honesty and religious society. He supported the saints and encouraged everyone, aiming them towards Christian holiness and purity. Many times he said when accepting young people into the church, "Now boys and girls, let six feet of earth cover before shaming the good name you have accepted today!" And he showed by word and action, that he did not like to hear of the death of the ungodly, but wanted everyone to come away from it and live.

At a period when there was lack of success he would say in his own pleasant manner when addressing his listeners, "My brother James Davies and myself have been for very many long years together, like two old fingerposts pointing you towards heaven, but to hell many of you are going despite all our efforts."

CHAPTER 9
ORIGINAL TO THE END

We have heard before now about some rich tightfisted ministers, but we will not now look into this subject. It cannot be known how far the miserliness and meanness of some churches towards their ministers, has driven some of them to be excessively frugal and cautious. Yes, without doubt, the cruelty of many churches towards their ministers and their families, has caused many, in their fear of poverty, to make them over-friendly with 'the unjust Mammon,' and to go in mental worry at times to forbidden land in their reasoning and their conscience, and because of this dampen down their hopes, kill their usefulness, hurt their lawful comforts for ever. But these things never worried Dafydd Evans very much at any time. Throughout the time he lived at Troedyrhiw he did not receive one halfpenny for preaching, and he was proverbial in his kindness towards other ministers of the Word. Troedyrhiw was the lodging house of the travellers in the Cwmduad and Ffynnon in those day; and many tired after their journey and wet through from the rain, found rest and comfortable lodgings under his homely and amusing home. Troedyrhiw was a pleasant haven following the rough journey, and a warm house after a stormy, wet journey over Llangeler Moor, or through Cwmdwyfran; and rather than the Ffynnon kept Dafydd Evans, it was Dafydd Evans who supported Ffynnon, and in this light we can understand what he had to say to young members on being admitted to the church. "You are expected," he said, "to keep the things of this house in the house, because they belong to the house. If you see anyone desirous of the bread of children tell him to come here to get it. Also, you are expected to contribute towards the cause in this chapel because the Lord wants you to succeed; not so much this or that much of the pound, like the church's tithe, but this much or that much for the Lord to succeed, and you will not find a cheaper religion anywhere than in Ffynnon, unless you go immediately to the Parish Church. It is nearly free in Ffynnon, and has nothing to do with the 'tenth'. This was as much as he was concerned because at that time he did not receive any money for preaching. Before he got married his father was not willing for him to accept any payment for preaching the gospel; after he was married until his release from prison, he did nor receive a farthing from the chapel.

He was very liberal and free towards the poor and needy, and his hand always ready to support Jesus Christ. The church at Llandeilo was in difficulty, and some of the members came to Dafydd Evans to tell him about the problem, and he lent them one hundred pounds, and never wanted it back unless he really needed it. Mrs. Evans grumbled because he gave so much to others. "O", he would say, "I am duty bound to help the cause of the Son of God to become free." And when he was offered payment he would say, "No, no, I will in all honesty not accept it, I will not receive interest from Jesus Christ in the form of money, you never know how much to give, and I don't know whether one hundred pounds for eternal life is enough; I will have the answer myself before long, and He can settle with me then. Later on he was in need of one hundred pounds, and as the reader knows, it is most unlikely that he ever received it; and what he did receive came from the collection in the churches he visited, and it seems that some were not over generous to him. He gave this money away, like any other money he had been given, and did not keep any record of what he had been given. He was as unthinking and innocent with regard to such matters, and his whole faith and world was in his religion, without possibly giving any consideration whether there was a great difference between the religion itself and people who say they are religious, and that no man or body of men who professed religion strongly enough did not ask for a receipt for a sum of money, but he believed that everyone was as honest as himself, but in this he was often disappointed, and reminded that he was surrounded by sinners. During periods when things were difficult for him financially he only received a pittance for his work. No larger sum for his ministry ever reached him other than thirteen pounds ten shillings, and this 'on a tide of the sea of generosity' when he was close to landing in the country of eternal plenty. I am not accusing the church at Ffynnon of being miserly, nor of being disrespectful towards him; no, they doted on him, and they would raise him now if they could from his grave.

Dafydd Evans never thought of leaving Fynnon. It would be the same to get him to leave as attempting to move the Frenni Fawr from its foundations. He was far too fond of his birthplace to give any consideration whatsoever of leaving, and would hardly be able to fit in to any other place, except the place nature and grace had placed him; and he was able to keep body and soul as neighbours, and raise a big family in spite of everything.

Towards the end of his life, Ffynnon members, and members of other churches in the district presented him with a testimonial. They wanted to show him their respect for him, and to pay tribute to him as a man, Christian and preacher, as well as to ease 'his pillow and make up the bed of his old age;' but it was for him like many of the earthly benefactors too late. Before he was able to enjoy some of the generosity of his fellow beings he had escaped far from the adversities of this life:-

In the meantime he was called home to receive an acknowledging testimonial from his Big Master - a testimonial that is really worth having, and all should be ambitious for it in the form of 'the perpetual crown of glory.' He was very useful for a long time working in the vineyard. His day had been long, and worked on until late. His battle had been long, and he carried the sword right up until the end. Rarely has anyone held it as long. He had been minister for fifty-five years, forty three of which he had spent preaching. And one thing that is strange, he preached even when he was eighty-three years old as he did when he was forty. Usually it is otherwise; the popular preachers standard of preaching deteriorates towards the "Marshes of Moab" on a "Tiresome day".

The art fades but the 'nature of talent keeps young in old age, and the greenery under a whitening crown.' Dafydd Evans' talent kept youthful the other side of eighty. His youth restored like the eagle - he was fired with enthusiasm and full of vigor. Even in the vale of death, his skill burnt fiercely until it licked the dark waters of Jordan!

Dafydd Evans died in exactly the same way as he lived - humorous, original, mindful and honest, and looked upon himself as a sinner, and thought a great deal of Jesus Christ as his Saviour, and his precious blood like medicine to clean him from his corruption and faults. About two years before his end he had been confined to his house and bed, and paralysed on one side due to a stroke. Someone asked him, "How are you, Mr. Evans" "O," he replied, "one side of me has died, and the other will also when it becomes ready." James Davies was also dying at the beginning of his illness, and one of his neighbours asked him, "Do you want me to say anything to James Davies?" "Tell him," he replied, "to hurry up or I'll be home before him." He often experienced doubts about his state, and was not on the best of terms with himself as a sinner. One day, while in bed, he was heard say to himself, "You poor creature!" you are thinking that you will have a crown, a throne and palm leaves! Yes indeed, you would make a proper king you old ungodly sinner! Yes indeed, you have always been ungodly - you were born ungodly - raised ungodly, ungodly you were when you were accepted into the church - ungodly you were as a preacher - ungodly you will die, and you will be ungodly at the day of judgment, you shall see." These utterances although strange, smells strongly of his honesty; because what would it take a heretic to talk to himself in such a way. He would be too frightened, in case a voice would be heard to say, "Very true! very true!"

On a visit to a friend he expressed doubts, but his friend reassured him of what he had said at the funeral of 'Malen Dywyll' - Dark Malen. I have already mentioned Malen, and that she was godly, and Dafydd Evans said in her funeral, "Malen must definitely be in heaven, yes indeed, she is bound to be in heaven; if she went to hell she would not stay there five minutes because the first thing she would do would be to shout for Jesus Christ at the top of her voice, and Beelzebub would tell two or three of his servants, "Throw this old woman out, she will not on any account be allowed to stay here, I could not stand her, throw her out this minute." His friend reminded him of the above saying of his, and he went quiet with a satisfactory smile, and said, "That Malen is without doubt in heaven, and I hope to be there with her soon."

In February, when the breeze was keen, moaning and very cold, and the snow fell softly on earth, one of the most lively of all creatures of the sons of women was dying in Cynwyl Elfed, and nearly ready to emigrate from the land of the ice and snow to the land of eternal summers. Through the window he could see the snow falling, and in his usual lively imagination he said, "Well, well, the snow is covering the earth and mountains today. It is covering the top of Frenni Fawr and Foel Cwmcerwin however high they are. Where are my big sins? O thanks! They have been covered although they are much higher than the highest mountain of the world. To God be the glory!" The day before he died he asked for his son John to come to him, and said to him, "Well, it is the end today, my boy," John replied, "What's the matter?" "O, I am dying, I am dying!" he said. "How do you feel?" John asked. "O, I feel great, but the old body wants to go to Ffynnon, and remember to bury me the other side of the stream that runs through the graveyard. Don't bury me on this side, it is too full already. There is not near enough room in the 'big bed', and what if you buried the old creature like me there?

Bury me the other side under the holly. Shon the cobbler says that he is to be buried at that spot. But surely, I am meant to be there. Be careful, be careful in case you do it differently. Do you promise, John, that you will see to it that it will be done?" "Of course I do, my dear father, but you haven't died yet." "Well, I am not completely dead yet, but I will be dead tomorrow."

He spoke the truth, because the following day, the fifth of March 1866, what was only the body of Dafydd Evans, Ffynnonhenry died, and was buried with reverence and deep sorrow according to his wishes in the graveyard of his dear Ffynnonhenry, on the 'other side', under the holly, and there he lies, and that until the great day, when and where the ungodly in their restlessness, and the weary, rest. And there is September of the same year he was followed to the 'predestined house' by his dear wife, and on the grave a beautiful memorial, and written on it the following words:- "To the memory of the Rev. Dafydd Evans, Minister of this church for 55 years, who died March 5 1866, aged 88 years. Also to the memory of Margaret, wife of the Rev. Dafydd Evans, who died September 27 1866, aged 68 years. Erected by his friends."

And if ever, dear reader, you go to Fynnonhenry graveyard, and looked over his grave, always remember that you will be standing over the grave of one of the most humorous of nature's children that ever decorated the human body - a lump of gold from nature's mine that had been polished by 'the grace of glory,' - the complete Welshman, without a drop of foreign blood in his veins, nor foreign savour in his clothes, only the product of the land where he was born, and the true, usage of the country in which he lived, and without doubt he was one of the best examples of an old original Welshman of 'the agreeable red blood' that had been made better by Divine grace, that showed heaven itself. I stood one day above his grave, and a tear ran down my cheek, realizing I was standing over the grave of one of the greatest characters, after searching high and low in Wales; it did not leave such a one to come after him, and his kind will not be found again; we did not, and we will not get only one Dafydd Evans, Ffynnonhenry, and thanks for one, this one who was worth many others, and we will not be happy until we meet him in heaven. Around his grave there played a lament, a song, grief and happiness, and tears and laughter in turn.

Not very often do we see a grave that makes one laugh, and to be amused in a graveyard, but that is how it is standing above Dafydd Evans' grave, and I doubt if angels managed to carry him all the way without laughing; I could almost hear them saying occasionally, "You must keep quiet, or we'll have to put you down." From the earthly home where his body lay, I was taken on that wing of faith to a splendid, pure soul, and I could see him standing before the throne of God's Lamb, throwing his crown at the feet of the one who had been nailed (to a cross), and in his unique manner shouting, "Hallelujah! Hallelujah! Blessed for ever with such an expensive salvation!" in a way that was never done by anyone before, or draw the attention of the holy throng, and raise for the second time their pleasure in praising the 'Middle Man;' and we had a glimpse of him afterwards surrounded by angels, and the spirit of the righteous, and the outstanding spirit of the 'Welsh fathers', in one of the houses of heaven on the shores of the 'living water,' where he entertains and blesses them when telling them of the 'path of life' and his original impressions of his new home, this in the language of heaven.

And we were awakened from a sweet and rare dream, leaving our subject under the everlasting crown of victory, and finding ourselves with the sword still in our hands, and the enemy utterly beaten, and there broke on to our ears the pleasant sound that we had never heard before - it was so sweet that even the enemies uproar ended, while he said, "Look, I am coming in a hurry; hold on to what you have, so that no one will steal your crown. The one that conquers, he is the one who will be dressed in gowns of white; and I will not erase his name from the book of life, but will confess before my Father, and before His angels."

REFLECTION

There have been many Christian biographies written of the saints of old but none quite like this one and I confess to you that you have only had an abridged version of the recorded account concerning Dafydd Evans, the half has not been told, this is due to a number of considerations. Firstly, for anyone to enjoy the full account, the reader would have to be almost as eccentric as the subject himself. Another reason, to quote the writer of Ecclesiastes, "of making of many books there is no end and much study is wearisome to the flesh", with the adding of stories upon stories with so many tales it was my personal view that a subtraction of the many humorous accounts is actually a plus in deriving the most profitable and best lessons concerning this true child of God.

I also took the liberty to divide the work into chapters and rearranged some of the material into some order as the original work of Benjamin Thomas consists of one paragraph of free thought of over fifty thousand words. The joy has been mine and I thank God for putting the original idea to Cyril Treharne to translate this work, to which God has used in shaping my mind and giving insights to the preachers and preaching of old.

People have an impact on us and it is my hope that in the reading of this account God will use it to be a means of some spiritual edification. What you will find is that many spiritual gems would have been slipped into your soul without you even realising, as you are taken up with very homely and humours anecdotes but then when you finish you realise that you have been learning the lessons that Dafydd Evans learned from the ordinary things around and that your eyes are a little bit more open to seeing God at work in the small everyday occurrence taken for granted, yet are filled with big spiritual truths.

Take the thrilling fact that God can and does use such people like Dafydd Evans, with all his oddities, for His work and service, many came to faith through his ministry and all one can say is to God be all the glory. His life highlights to us, although not formally educated in the schools of this world, he was truly learned and in touch with the great truths of the gospel and with the common graces of life from which he was able to feed a people for fifty years of ministry and was second to none concerning spiritual matters.

He was equipped by God with a knowledge of divine things, understanding of how people and life works, a judgement concerning the cares of the Church and a wisdom which was not found from books. He instinctively knew and was able to discern, for example, how one preacher who came was not called of God, neither was he placed there by the devil but was self-appointed, self-called which Dafydd Evans so clearly discerned. Again, how Dafydd could discern between two types of preachers, one who needed the wind behind them and the other who would bring you to shore even if the wind was not present and many other gems in his pastoring of people. He was a Shephard of God's sheep who knew the flock and the flock knew him and in preaching he could hold the attention of the sleepiest congregation.

But there are two other thoughts this work can teach us, one is to consider how it is that such a book became a national best seller, being sold in its thousands, going into many editions, this was the go-to biography of the Baptist non-conformity in the year 1870. An interest which is hard for us to imagine these days, the place of the Preacher in Wales had in the heart of the people of God. Preachers were household names and pictures of Ministers would be found hanging on the walls of many a home, there was a reverence for the office, no matter how humble the cause and there was a hunger to know the story of how God worked through his chosen instruments. What is interesting in this account is that it was not filled with super spiritual accounts of a false piety to which many Christian biographies have fallen foul and as a result produced a false ideal which is not truly biblical, any one who knows the welsh non-conformist mind of that day would relate to the earthliness of the clay vessel in which the power of God was found.

Yet, what is also highlighted, and is a cause of concern, is the lack of doctrinal solid teaching. There are reasons for this failing, it was written in a style which was simply readable, people are more engaged with personalities rather than precepts and principles and with Dafydd Evans the best of material was in the writer's hand. It is not that doctrinal truths concerning the person of Christ, the place of Scripture, the atoning blood of the Saviour, the forgiveness of sins, new birth, heaven and hell, have been left out, all these subjects are touched upon taking for granted that the Non-Conformist audience accepted these beliefs without question. Wales spiritually was in a far healthier condition than today, where religious talk with biblical narrative was the conversation of the village, the mart, the town. Yet at the same time this book highlights the need and perhaps the weakness which had already set into the heart of the Welsh pew and pulpit, it was the act of preaching and not the preaching of the Word itself which became the focus of many a congregation in the nation.

Nerveless, Dafydd Evans was blessed by God, he was Calvinistic in his doctrine and a devoted and committed servant to the truth of the Gospel. Benjamin Thomas knew this and Benjamin Thomas himself had an agenda in the writing of this work, not only for keeping the memory of Dafydd Evans alive but also to bring before the Welsh constituency just how God had worked in the past and with what God used to bring Him glory. And in this work Benjamin Thomas makes this case, by highlighting the originality of Dafydd Evans in contrast to others who had learning and training in the ministry but lacked the power and life which Dafydd Evans had and who was used of God.

An issue had risen in the denomination at the time which concerned ministerial training being moved out of the academies and into the universities, so that the ministry would be more accommodating to gain a greater acceptance and credibility in the ministering of the gospel of God. The fact is, that God so often chooses the foolish things of the world to confound the wise. With Dafydd Evans, a point was being made that God uses those who are not shaped by the mould of political correctness, or simply to what had become the respectability of Chapel life, particularly in the cities. God still has his Elijah's and John the Baptist who were given supernatural understanding and insight into spiritual things that is somehow missed by the most trained theological student.

If this was a concern of Benjamin Thomas in his day, how much more needed today with the media age where perfect presentation is everything where the message comes over dead right, politically correct, poetically delightful and exegetically perfect but with no power.

A case could be made for Dafydd Evans, being one of the most eccentric preachers of the Welsh pulpit in a land which has been known for its characters from all walks of life, Dafydd Evans, head and shoulders above all. God made him an original and his environment, upbringing and personal history added to the unconventional manner of his personality and ministry. He was made and shaped by God for a work to be carried out among ordinary country people, he was an instrument in the Master's hand for over 54 years, preaching the good news of Jesus Christ to lost sinners, the atoning death of the Son of God at Calvary and His great conquering victory from the grave.

It shows us that God loves His Church and does raise up for His flock even in the most unpromising of places, small and forgotten and off the beaten track, God met with a people and a community and they knew of salvation and new birth, they knew in such places as Ffynnonhenry the working of the Holy Spirit's power on the preaching and truth that prophets and righteous men longed to see and know.

May this book in the simple and homely read cause the hearts of many to pray that God will be so gracious to us once again in this land, that every village, every town and every city would know not only the gospel but of gospel preachers and shepherds, even in the most remote places of this land. Now to God be all the glory. Amen.